LIVE MORE THINK LESS

Overcoming Depression and Sadness with Metacognitive Therapy

DR PIA CALLESEN

In collaboration with

ANNE METTE FUTTRUP

Translated by Anna George

ICON

First published in the UK in 2020
by Icon Books Ltd, Omnibus Business Centre,
39–41 North Road, London N7 9DP
email: info@iconbooks.com
www.iconbooks.com

This edition published in the UK in 2020 by Icon Books Ltd

Sold in the UK, Europe and Asia
by Faber & Faber Ltd, Bloomsbury House,
74–77 Great Russell Street,
London WC1B 3DA or their agents

Distributed in the UK, Europe and Asia
by Grantham Book Services, Trent Road, Grantham NG31 7XQ

Distributed in the USA
by Publishers Group West,
1700 Fourth Street, Berkeley, CA 94710

Distributed in Australia and New Zealand
by Allen & Unwin Pty Ltd,
PO Box 8500, 83 Alexander Street,
Crows Nest, NSW 2065

Distributed in South Africa
by Jonathan Ball, Office B4, The District,
41 Sir Lowry Road, Woodstock 7925

Distributed in India by Penguin Books India,
7th Floor, Infinity Tower – C, DLF Cyber City,
Gurgaon 122002, Haryana

Distributed in Canada by Publishers Group Canada,
76 Stafford Street, Unit 300
Toronto, Ontario M6J 2S1

ISBN: 978-178578-668-6

Typeset in Baskerville MT by Marie Doherty

Printed and bound in Great Britain
by Clays Ltd, Elcograf S.p.A.

LIVE MORE THINK LESS

NOTE FROM THE AUTHOR

If you suffer from severe depression, you should seek medical advice. You cannot be healed by reading and implementing the exercises in this book. This book cannot replace a course of metacognitive therapy at an MCT-I-registered clinic or with an MCT-I certified therapist, but it will give you inspiration and ideas for a new way out of dark thoughts and depression.

CONTENTS

ABOUT THE AUTHOR

Dr Pia Callesen is a therapist and specialist in metacognitive therapy, having trained at the MCT Institute in Manchester with Professor Adrian Wells, the originator of MCT. She completed her PhD at Manchester University and works as a therapist and clinic manager in Denmark. She has written two popular books on metacognitive therapy, *Live More Think Less* and *Seize Life, Let Go of Anxiety*, which have both been bestsellers in Denmark and are now published in multiple languages across the world. Her study into the effectiveness of metacognitive therapy for depression, published in *Scientific Reports* in 2020, suggests that MCT has considerable benefits which may exceed those of cognitive behavioural therapy (CBT). Her clinic, Cektos, offers online therapy in English.

'Everyone has negative thoughts, and everyone believes their negative thoughts sometimes. But not everyone develops depression or emotional suffering.'

ADRIAN WELLS

FOREWORD

By Pia Callesen

For decades, established psychotherapists have held firm to the assumption that depression is a biological disease of the brain and that symptoms of depression are primarily caused by a lack of the neurotransmitter serotonin. As a result, for many years many therapists have prescribed medication – so-called 'happy pills' – as the first step when patients have presented with depressive symptoms. Patients may also have been offered a consultation with a psychologist or psychotherapist trained in conversational therapy. The purpose of these conversations has been, in many cases, to map and process problems and trauma or to turn negative thoughts into more positive or realistic thoughts.

However, groundbreaking new research shows that depression is a condition that can largely be controlled by the individual themselves. Several studies – including my own PhD from Manchester University, completed at the end of 2016 – illustrate that depression occurs when we deal with negative thoughts and feelings in inappropriate ways and that we can, therefore, reduce the risk of melancholy and depression by learning to relate to our negative thoughts and feelings in a more appropriate way.

In this book I address the obsolete understanding of depression as an uncontrollable state which affects us, and which we ourselves have no influence over. I also address the equally outdated treatment methods, year-long conversational therapies and medicine, and instead introduce a new and very effective method. It is called metacognitive therapy.

Metacognitive therapy was developed by British psychologist and professor Adrian Wells from Manchester University, based on 25 years of research into why some people develop mental illnesses, including depression, while others do not. When Wells presented his treatment manuals, he documented that it is not grief, accidents, sad feelings or negative thoughts that makes us depressed. Rather what makes us depressed is how we deal with our thoughts. When we ruminate – when we contemplate and let our thoughts go round and round for hours each day – we are at a greater risk of developing depression than if we were to passively observe our thoughts and let them be.

Wells also found that there are three main underlying reasons as to why some of us ruminate more than others: first, we are not aware that we are ruminating; second, we don't believe we can control our ruminations; and third, we are convinced that our ruminations help us. When we constantly monitor our own well-being and check in as to how we are doing with one thing or another, we lead ourselves into a downward spiral that can cause and maintain symptoms of depression such as sadness and lack of energy. This still applies even if we try to think rationally, positively or in a caring manner towards ourselves. All these ways of dealing with thoughts create more thoughts. As Wells says, 'You cannot overcome the problem of overthinking with more thinking – you can only overcome it by thinking less.' Metacognitive therapy was tailored from his research into this.

I have been a psychologist since the beginning of the millennium and the first decade of my practice involved traditional cognitive behavioural therapy (CBT), which is one of the most tried and tested and well-documented methods in the world. Cognitive therapy is based on the idea that thoughts are central to our well-being and, therefore, need to be processed and changed in order to overcome depression and anxiety.

My introduction to metacognitive therapy – and to Adrian Wells – radically changed my understanding of mental illnesses. After a case study of hundreds of clients in metacognitive therapy, it was clear to me: the cause of mental illnesses is not, as I had believed for ten years, a combination of genetic heritage, environment and negative thoughts. The cause, as Wells describes, is flawed mental and behavioural strategies. We become depressed because we tackle our thoughts and beliefs in inappropriate ways. Therefore, depression is not a disease we have to live with.

This realisation created a tsunami of thoughts within my mind: could I have been much more helpful to my clients over the years? Many of my clients felt that cognitive therapy had been helpful, but I now discovered that with metacognitive therapy I could both reduce treatment time and significantly increase the effect of the treatment.

Shortly after being introduced to Wells and metacognitive therapy, I personally needed therapeutic help. My husband

and I had just become parents to a little boy, and the doctors gave us the unhappy news that our little Louie had been born with a rare genetic defect which caused epileptic seizures. The seizures would damage his brain if we didn't get them under control. I was shaken to my core and deeply unhappy, and thoughts whirled in my head: What would happen to Louie? How would my husband and I deal with things in the future if Louie became very brain damaged? What about all our hopes and dreams?

I felt a great urge to do my own research as well as ask the doctors questions, so that I could learn everything about my son's genetic defect. I wanted to be a super-mother, problem-solver and expert in the field. But my new knowledge of metacognitive therapy helped me limit these contemplations. It wasn't my place to use all my mental power to find solutions and heal Louie. It was the doctors'. I wasn't going to think myself into a depressive state. Instead, I was going to be a mother who was there for Louie and a wife who supported her husband.

I decided to leave be the many thoughts and questions that arose throughout the day. So, I set a fixed time from 5 to 6pm, when I could contemplate and ruminate. As one of my colleagues observes, it's like having a piece of chewing gum sitting in your mouth all day and only being allowed to start chewing it at 5 o'clock. This is not easy. It requires awareness, patience and determination to learn to let go of thoughts and to shift your focus to other areas of your life. But I experienced first-hand just how powerful metacognitive therapy is, and all three of us, Louie, my husband and I, came through the crisis unscathed.

My wish for readers of this book is that they – like me – realise that it is possible to control the strategies that either create or maintain depression. This book describes the phases of metacognitive therapy step by step, and at each step I show how I employ these methods in my clinic, and what exercises and tips my clients use when implementing metacognitive principles in their lives.

The book cannot replace a course of metacognitive treatment. If you are very depressed, I would recommend you seek immediate medical advice so that you get the best treatment for you. If you are very depressed, metacognitive therapy can still help. Trials on individuals have shown that attention training alone, which is part of metacognitive therapy (see Chapter 3), significantly relieves the symptoms of deeply depressed people. For a list of MCT-I registered therapists, please see page 169.

You will meet Natacha, Mette, Leif and Berit in this book, all of whom were depressed in relation to major life crises, which naturally led to negative thoughts and feelings. These four share their stories first-hand: their problems; how they felt down and depressed; and how they, through metacognitive therapy, developed a new relationship with their thoughts and feelings so that today each of them is free from depression.

Metacognitive therapy is not a safeguard against life's challenges. It is a tool for rediscovering control over contemplations and ruminations and for shifting focus to other areas of life beyond ourselves. That's where we overcome depression and where life is lived.

FOREWORD

By Adrian Wells, University of Manchester, UK

There is a need for more effective evidence-based psychological therapies. In this book Dr Pia Callesen describes the use of metacognitive therapy (MCT) in her clinic. Dr Callesen is a graduate of the Metacognitive Therapy Institute (www.mct-institute.com) and also completed a PhD under my supervision at the University of Manchester. She conducted a major trial of the effectiveness of MCT compared with cognitive behavioural therapy in people suffering from depression.

In this book the reader can find an overview of MCT richly illustrated with the experiences of patients who have completed treatment. The book will be an invaluable resource for people suffering from depression who wish to consider this new treatment approach, and for anyone interested in an introduction to some of the key principles.

Metacognitive therapy is concerned with how a person regulates thinking. No matter if life is bad or good, an individual can learn to reduce thinking patterns that cause depression. MCT is grounded in advances in psychological research and theory that a colleague and I set out in 1994. In that work we made some radical claims for the time. Backed by research, we identified that most problems of anxiety and depression are caused by a thinking pattern that is linked to a person's underlying (metacognitive) belief system. If we could remove that thinking pattern and modify that belief system, then we would have a new type of therapy and perhaps more effective outcomes. After years of research and clinical work I developed MCT to do this. A large amount of data has accumulated supporting this approach.

Dr Callesen's book will have achieved its aims if it motivates sufferers of depression and also therapists to find out more about MCT. It will have succeeded if it brings hope and signposts an escape route from the personal suffering that depression brings.

Chapter 1

NO MORE ENDLESS
SELF-ANALYSIS

Do you know the expression 'to be hit by depression'?
Well, I'm going to provoke you with an assertion: we are not *hit* by depression. It doesn't come from the outside. We ourselves provoke it. Therefore, we ourselves can also fight it if we want to. We can take control so that depressive thoughts don't take control of us.

It may be hard for you to believe this. Most of us have learned that depression is a condition that strikes us either because of an emotional crisis or because of a chemical imbalance in the brain. There is no avoidance of depression in these assumptions. It is nothing we can effect. We have learned that depression arises according to the situation – no matter how we handle it.

Despite this being a commonplace and firm opinion, new research shows that this is not how depression works. We all get scrapes and scratches on our bodies and souls throughout life. We experience crises, defeats, illnesses and disappointments. And we feel pain, grief, fear, sadness, frustration and anger. But we don't all become depressed. Why not? The answer is found in those strategies we each use whenever we face a crisis and negative thoughts. Some strategies are so inappropriate that they lead us straight into depression. Others lead us past depression – we can learn these strategies and help ourselves. These strategies comprise metacognitive therapy.

When I tell my clients that they can take responsibility for easing their depression, some experience it as a lot of pressure. 'Is it now my own responsibility to get better?' they ask. I want to assure you that it's quite normal to find it difficult in the beginning. But I would also like to assure that you can do it with the right help. Later in the book you will meet Natacha, Mette, Leif and Berit, who after just six to twelve sessions of metacognitive therapy all recovered from depression.

With metacognitive therapy, we finally get rid of the remains of ancient Freudian psychoanalysis, which believed that talking about childhood experiences was the way to treat depression. We also challenge cognitive therapy, which seeks to change the negative beliefs a depressed person holds into more realistic or nuanced beliefs. Metacognitive therapy, which neither scapegoats childhood nor alters dark thoughts to brighter versions, is a groundbreaking paradigm shift within psychology. With it, endless self-analysis is no longer the way to break free from depression. This form of therapy is based on doing *less*, not *more* with your thoughts and feelings.

Understandably, people who have participated in other forms of therapy can perceive metacognitive therapy as a 'reverse' form of therapy. Because when we seek therapy, we have an expectation that to get better we need to process our problems and talk through our feelings.

Metacognitive therapy, on the other hand, starts with the premise that extensive processing of your thoughts and feelings gives rise to symptoms of depression. If we spend several hours a day thinking about, talking about, processing and analysing our negative experiences and feelings, or if we grapple with finding solutions to our emotional issues, we risk ruminating ourselves into depression. When we fall into symptoms of depression or a depressive state, we give ourselves even more to contemplate – namely the depression itself – and with lots of analysis and thought processing about the depression we are at risk of keeping it alive.

SURPRISING RESEARCH RESULTS

Metacognitive therapy is currently taking the world by storm with its proven effect on depression. The treatment has been cited in National Health Service guidelines in the UK as a treatment to consider for generalised anxiety. I am convinced that we will soon see similar recommendations for the treatment of depression and anxiety in other countries.

It was actually the mention of other researchers' and psychologists' promising results within metacognitive therapy that made me decide to combine my clinical work with research. I was deeply inspired by the research published by Professor Adrian Wells: 70–80 per cent of people in metacognitive therapy recovered from anxiety or depression. This is a significantly higher result than with other therapeutic forms, including cognitive therapy. However, the positive results were based primarily on small-scale studies and trials. I was curious to find out whether or not metacognitive therapy could produce equally strong results when applied to a target group in my clinic. So, I wrote to Wells about starting a PhD project. We planned to carry out a series of so-called effectiveness trials among the people seeking help in my clinic. In other words, I was going to investigate the direct effect of the therapy.

First, I conducted a systematic review of all the research into the effect of therapeutic treatment on depression. This revealed that about 50 per cent of participants in the described studies recovered from depression using methods such as cognitive therapy and other therapies which focus on a client's thoughts, current life circumstances and relationships with other people. Fifty per cent is not a statistic to shout about.

Next, I set out to investigate whether or not the impressive results achieved by Wells could be reproduced with Danes. My investigation was to be conducted first as single-client trials and later as a larger scale randomised trial. In concrete terms this meant that in the weeks prior to the therapy session, I measured the participants' level of depression several times to ensure that any effect was not just based on the passing of time. A colleague and I then offered metacognitive therapy to four Danes suffering from depression, under the supervision of Adrian Wells.

All four were deeply depressed at the beginning. Three recovered from depression after 5–11 sessions of MCT while one remained mildly depressed. Six months later, all four participants indicated that they were now free from depression – maintaining the effect. The results were impressive, and the trial is now published in the *Scandinavian Journal of Psychology*.

After the single-client trial, I completed a larger study over six years of more than 150 depressed Danes, whom I randomly divided into two groups: one group received cognitive therapy, while the other received metacognitive therapy. The study left no doubt: metacognitive therapy had a significantly better effect – in both the short and long term. Parallel to my research, a group of Norwegian researchers, headed by psychologist Roger Hagen, studied the effect of metacognitive therapy on 39 depressed Norwegians. Again, the results were outstanding. Between 70 and 80 per cent recovered, and at a follow-up assessment six months later, the same number of participants were still free from depression. The results from these studies document that metacognitive therapy has – at present – probably the best observed effect against depression.

ARE YOU IN COGNITIVE THERAPY?

If you are in cognitive therapy or other forms of therapy and would like to continue with that method, I would not recommend you use the principles of metacognitive therapy at the same time as these methods can negate each other's effect. Metacognitive therapy works best in its pure form.

THE MIND REGULATES ITSELF

As mentioned earlier, therapists have suggested that depression and other mental illnesses hit us externally when life is painful. Treatment methods have, as a result, focussed on processing the traumas and bad experiences believed to have accumulated in a person's mind. This was repeated in therapeutic circles when Adrian Wells and his colleague Gerald Matthews presented an entirely new model of the human mind in the early 1990s, after many years of research. They documented that, as a rule, the mind regulates itself; just as our body can often heal itself, so too can our psyche.

Over thousands of years, the human body has developed the ability to heal wounds and bones after cuts and breaks. We all learn early in childhood that a bloody knee after a fall from a bike doesn't continue to bleed for the rest of our lives. It is cured in the most wonderful way, without us having to do anything ourselves, and it happens relatively quickly. But if we pick, scratch and rub at the wound, then it won't knit together. On the contrary, we risk making things worse by creating infection and scar tissue.

The same happens in our psyche, as Wells and Matthews' research demonstrates. In the aftermath of an unpleasant or unhappy experience, such as a divorce, accident or fire, thoughts will naturally focus on this experience. The experience will appear in our mind again and again, several times a day, in the form of thoughts and images. It is natural that these thoughts and feelings will be negative and dominated by grief, fear, sadness, disappointment and perhaps even anger.

Immediately after the bad experience, the psyche will hurt and suffer – exactly like a knee when the skin is scratched off. In the same way that our knee will heal if we resist picking at it, so too will our mind if we refrain from fostering feelings by ruminating on them. Thoughts, images and impulses visit us briefly but will disappear again if we don't grab them, suppress them or otherwise try to deal with them. If we don't keep them in the front of our mind for regular access, they will pass through like grains of sand in a sieve.

This new understanding puts an end to the earlier perception of the causes of depression. Because if we take the mind being able to heal itself as the starting point, then why do some people become depressed after a life crisis while others don't?

THE MIND WORKS ON THREE LEVELS

Wells challenged the widespread perception that unprocessed negative experiences contribute to depression. He explained that everyone has negative thoughts sometimes, and everyone occasionally believes these negative thoughts, but not everyone develops a mental illness. Therefore, Wells and Matthews posed the question: if having negative experiences and thoughts does not in itself lead to depression, what does? What are the underlying factors that make a person depressed?

Their research led to a metacognitive model of the human mind. The *S-REF model* (Self-Regulatory Executive Function Model of Emotional Disorder) shows that the mind operates on three levels:

1. A lower level that is constantly hit by impulses, thoughts and feelings. If we don't engage these impulses, thoughts and feelings, then they are fleeting and disappear again by themselves.

2. A middle strategic level where we choose our strategies for dealing with our thoughts.

3. An upper, metacognitive level that contains our knowledge of possible strategies.

Let's look at these levels in greater detail.

1. Lower level: automatic thoughts and images

At this level we are constantly being hit by impulses, thoughts, images, feelings, memories and metacognitive beliefs about ourselves, which our brain is built to produce thousands of. We can't control all these thoughts, associations and impulses coming. They are natural and arise unconsciously from encounters, events and experiences – both good and not so good. For instance, if you have been disappointed and hurt by a romantic partner whom you loved, you will naturally feel nervous and unsure about entering into a new romantic relationship. Those kinds of automated thoughts and feelings, created by experiences earlier in life, are quite common and not a problem in themselves. It is the handling of these involuntary thoughts and feelings that determine our mood and well-being. How that handling occurs is decided at the middle strategic level.

HOW THE PSYCHE WORKS

Simplified and adapted from Wells and Matthews' S-REF Model, 1994

METACOGNITIVE BELIEFS LEVEL

'I can't control my ruminations.'
'I can ruminate to solutions and answers.'

MIDDLE STRATEGIC LEVEL

Strategies for dealing with thoughts

Ruminations, worries, attempts at rational/
compassionate/positive thinking, suppression of thoughts,
avoidance, monitoring mood and other checks

LOWER LEVEL

Automatic thoughts and images

The tens of thousands of thoughts and
inner sensory input that hit us every day

2. Middle level: strategies

This level contains our strategies for those thoughts and feelings that occur at the lower, uncontrollable level. The strategies determine whether or not thoughts and feelings are fleeting and transient, or whether they remain in our awareness, going around in circles. All active strategies for thoughts and feelings, such as rumination and worrying, sustain our stream of thoughts. We deal more or less consciously with the impulses from the lower level, using voluntary strategies which we choose from our metacognitive knowledge of both our way of thinking and our emotional life (our upper metacognitive beliefs level of the mind). For example, if you feel that you have lost the spark for your work, your strategy for dealing with this might be analysis. You then use your intellect to analyse your knowledge, encounters, events and experiences in order to explain the missing spark. You question what has changed. Perhaps it's time to change jobs? Find a completely new industry? Re-educate yourself? If your application of problem-solving strategies leads to a solution, then all is good and you move on with your life. But maybe those good analytical skills come up short. So, instead, the ruminations lead to more contemplations, which in turn occupy more and more hours every day: Can I afford to go back to college? Could I borrow against the house? Could we move into something cheaper? Would the children have to change school?

3. Metacognitive beliefs level: assumptions about our thoughts and thought processes

Here are the beliefs we turn to when deciding how to tackle our impulses, thoughts and feelings. As we think thousands of thoughts every day, we don't have time to deal with them all individually. Therefore, we need to make a choice and decide which thoughts we want to process and which we don't. For example, if we are fired from a job, we may find that it makes sense to ruminate on its cause: why was I fired? We believe that ruminations are useful, that we can think ourselves towards an explanation. Yet we might simultaneously feel that we can't control whether or not we are ruminating. Whether we ruminate for two or ten hours a day, it feels random and beyond our control. Our metacognitive beliefs determine whether we give in to rumination or whether we feel that we have a choice. So, the metacognitive beliefs level contains our knowledge of whether we believe we can turn on and off our handling of our thoughts and whether we believe we can control our strategies for our streams of thought.

I will demonstrate the S-REF model using the case of a female client who had just got divorced and had come to my clinic because she was in conflict with her ex-husband. They argued constantly about where the children should live, how they should be raised and whether they should be allowed to decide which parent they would stay with for major holidays. Every day she thought about whether or not her children were doing well when they were with their father. About whether he was treating them properly. About whether she was being a good mother, given she was the one who had decided to get divorced. All of these thoughts originated at the **lower level** in her mind as automatic thoughts.

She was astonished by these thoughts. Every day she promised herself that once the children had been put to bed in the evening she would sit down and find answers to all her questions by carefully thinking about or writing out her thoughts in a diary. These ruminations and strategic planning occurred at the **middle strategic level** of her mind.

She was convinced that she could not control her ruminations. She ruminated, unaware of how long she was ruminating, be it for an hour or ten hours a day. She was also convinced that this would help her if she just thought long enough – that the ruminations were actually useful. She processed the content of her thoughts in the hope of making them less painful and eventually, perhaps, making them disappear. She also hoped that by processing her thoughts she would come to believe that she was a good mother. These metacognitive beliefs pertaining to the ruminations being uncontrollable and useful are found at the **metacognitive beliefs level** of her mind.

OUR METACOGNITION KNOWS BEST

An example of a metacognitive experience that we are all familiar with is the 'tip of the tongue phenomenon', which we get a sense of when we are doing a crossword and need to find the word, for example, for a 'green gemstone': 'Oh, what's that called again?

I know it. It's on the tip of my tongue.' We know that we know the word. But for some reason we can't retrieve it from our memory bank. How can we know that we know the answer but yet be unable to think of it? This is because our brain, or our metacognition, has an overview of the knowledge it contains – even if we can't grasp it completely.

It is our middle strategic level that determines which strategies we choose to engage in order to extract the stored knowledge. Some people use a concentration strategy. They try to ruminate through to the stored knowledge by putting all their energy into thinking about the name of the green gemstone. Others use a more structured strategy like reviewing the entire alphabet in the attempt to find the name. Could it start with A? With B? With C? However, quite often the best strategy is actually to do as little as possible, to let the question be until this level of our mind has itself dived into the archives for an answer. Later – for example, while out for a walk – it will hit us: 'Jade! Jade is a green gemstone.'

The point is that most answers and solutions to our questions don't show up because we ruminate. Our metacognition does the work for us completely automatically.

SELF-ANALYSIS WILL MAKE YOU DEPRESSED

Many of us rack our brains trying to solve our problems. We believe that with the help of our thought processes and cognition we can force out the answers. But the best strategy when we need to remember something and apply knowledge is often, as I said, doing as little as possible. The answers will either appear by themselves at some point, or the questions will disappear and be forgotten because they weren't important.

Wells and colleagues discovered in their research that the same applies when we are melancholic, sad or depressed. If we use all our mental powers to ruminate, we risk maintaining the sad thoughts, thereby making our mood even worse. Therefore, it is best to let your thoughts be. We shouldn't try to force them away, but rather just passively observe their flow.

It is not the amount of unpleasant experiences and negative thoughts that leads to depression. Instead, Wells and Matthews ascertained that an attention syndrome known as *cognitive attentional syndrome* (CAS) was the primary cause of most mental illnesses, including depression.

In doing so, they also answered an earlier question: if the mind heals itself, why do some people become depressed after a life crisis while others don't? The answer is found in the amount of attention that we give to our thoughts about problems and life crises. Simply put: we ruminate ourselves into depression.

Cognitive attentional syndrome is not a classical syndrome as it doesn't contain a collection of symptoms like a syndrome usually does. Rather the syndrome is an umbrella term for four basic strategies that, when used excessively, strengthen our thoughts and feelings and can cause setbacks in the form of depression or other mental illnesses. The four strategies, which we'll elaborate on in a moment, are:

- Rumination

- Worry

- Monitoring behaviour

- Inappropriate coping behaviour (e.g. avoiding situations or resorting to excessive rest, sleep, alcohol and such like).

Let me be clear: all human beings naturally and inevitably have dark and negative thoughts that we sometimes ruminate on or worry about for a while. That is not a problem. Only when we develop a deep and long-term focus on the dark and negative thoughts do we risk becoming sad and provoking depression.

A common trait of all people with mental illnesses is an excessive use of one or more of these four strategies: spending many hours ruminating every day; worrying constantly; monitoring our mood over and over; or regularly dulling the thoughts with sleep, rest or substances like alcohol. This excessive focus is seen in everyone with a mental illness, but it is expressed differently from illness to illness. As a rule, depressed people tend to ruminate more than people with anxiety, who tend to worry more.

Does this mean that it is our own fault if we develop depression? Are we asking for it if we tend to worry or contemplate a lot? No, of course not. Nobody should feel guilty about having a mental illness. No one ruminates themselves into the dark on purpose. We all have our own ways of handling our thoughts and feelings. Most of us have inbuilt strategies that we developed in our youth. Essentially, we learn these strategies in one of two ways:

1. *We copy our parents or other people we look up to, or we do what those people tell us we should do.* For instance, some of us will be told by our parents that it is important to 'think long and hard' before making an important decision – such as choosing a partner or what to study. We will take this literally and will, therefore, spend many of our waking hours extensively overthinking.

2. *We learn by observing other people's reactions to our behaviour and by which behaviours help us to achieve what we want.* For example, if we have been rewarded for being highly analytical in school, we will reinforce this behaviour in other areas of life.

We can also learn new strategies throughout life, for example, through therapy. Metacognitive therapy helps us to identify our inappropriate strategies and replace them with appropriate ones.

The four basic, inappropriate strategies in cognitive attentional syndrome (we'll also refer to these as our 'CAS responses' later in the book) are generally aimed at solving problems, creating control or otherwise managing events in our lives. Everybody uses these strategies, and they aren't inherently destructive to us. When we ruminate on being fired from a job, we can call it reflection – we reflect on why we were fired. Did we do something wrong? If we worry about how our children will cope with our divorce, we can call it care. If we are sensitive to how we are actually feeling and allow ourselves to lie on the sofa after a divorce, we can call it taking care of ourselves. There is nothing wrong with that.

IT IS QUITE NATURAL TO BE SAD

Negative thoughts and sadness are natural for everyone and do not in themselves lead to depression. Only if you engage with your thoughts about your sadness – that is, deal with them and ruminate on them for a long time – can you risk developing symptoms of depression. According to medical criteria, you need to have had a number of symptoms for at least two weeks for a clinical diagnosis. If you are in a natural state of grief, for example, after the death of a loved one, the symptoms must last for at least two months before depression will be diagnosed.

The problem arises when we come to believe that these strategies are necessary for us and that we can neither control nor limit them. The time we spend thinking determines whether the thoughts remain an appropriate self-analysis or whether we end up overthinking and developing depression. There is a vast difference between analysing your thoughts and feelings for a single hour during the day, and spending twelve days ruminating and contemplating.

So, is it best to try to avoid completely ruminating, worrying, keeping checks on your mood and taking an extra rest on bad days? No, it is not. Of course we need to think about things and look inward to solve problems. We just shouldn't spend all our waking hours doing so.

You can see just how variable CAS can be in an example of two men who, after being made redundant from the same workplace during the same round of redundancies, supported each other. They both felt that the redundancy process had been very unpleasant, and both were filled with negative thoughts and feelings: 'Why was I let go? What is going on with management? Will I be able to get a new job when I've been wronged like this?' Both men's spouses were understanding and listened to them, and both men found comfort in their respective families, despite suffering from a feeling of having failed their wives and children by no longer being able to provide their income.

Soon, however, the behaviour of the two men began to differ. One decided to stop the endless ruminating once he realised it was maintaining his bad mood. He owed it to himself and to his family to get over it, he thought. The other man saw no other solution than to search for answers. The ruminations took over, creating new ruminations: 'Have I completely lost control of my thoughts? What is wrong with me?'

It's almost unnecessary to tell you that while one man moved on with his life in a new job, the other was diagnosed with depression and prescribed antidepressants. The only difference between the two was the length of the period spent ruminating.

Let's review the four elements of CAS in more detail.

Strategy no. 1:
RUMINATION

To 'ruminate' means to think about things over and over. Interestingly, the word stems from the Latin *rumen*, the name given to a compartment of a cow's stomach – where the expression 'chewing the cud' also comes from. Cows chew their food twice in order to digest it properly. We talk about something being 'food for thought' and having to 'digest an idea', but rumination – coming back to that thought repeatedly – can lead to feeling down and to symptoms of depression such as insomnia, a lack of energy, a lack of concentration, difficulty remembering or, in the worst case, to depression itself. There are three reasons why people start to ruminate:

1. We are unaware that we are ruminating;

2. We are convinced that we can't control our ruminations; or

3. We are convinced that such ruminating is useful.

Typical rumination starts with thoughts about what, why and how:

- What is wrong with me? What do I need to do to get rid of my depression?

- Why can't I make sense of anything? Why did I get depressed? Why can't I remember anything?

- How do I fix all my mistakes and deficiencies?

Strategy no. 2:
WORRY

Another strategy in CAS is worrying. For the vast majority of people, worries are just as natural a part of life as, say, joy. We worry about everything and anything: whether the rice pudding is too sweet; whether we remembered to lock the door; whether our newly licensed teenager is driving carefully; whether we'll lose our job in the next round of redundancies; whether we'll pass the exam; whether or not we are well liked by our colleagues. All these worries are normal and perfectly alright.

Worrying becomes a problematic mental activity when you dwell on certain thoughts. For instance, you might seize upon the idea of infidelity at a Christmas party – perhaps you saw this happen at your own workplace, or it featured in a TV show you watched – and you start worrying about whether your own spouse could be unfaithful at such festivities. If you get caught up in this worry, nurturing it to an exaggerated degree, you risk developing physical symptoms such as heart palpitations, a racing pulse and dizziness. The same physical reactions can be caused by worrying about more general anxieties about the future, for example: 'What if I get sick? What if I'm not allowed to participate in the project at work? What if I never get better?' If you seize upon such thoughts and worry a lot, you risk developing anxiety and symptoms of depression. If you have been feeling down for a long time or have been depressed, then you probably know the feeling that these worries go round in circles in your head. Perhaps you fear that the worries will never disappear.

In contrast to ruminations, worries typically form around hypothetical scenarios and so start with 'What if …' statements. For example:

- What if my brain gets damaged from depression?

- What if my family gets tired of me and my wife wants a divorce?

- What if I never get better?

Strategy no. 3:
MONITORING BEHAVIOUR

As with the previous two strategies, it is quite normal to pay attention to your mood once in a while. We can all feel whether we are happy, sad, dejected or in need of care. We all experience feeling sadder or more lethargic at some points in time, then wake up one morning to discover that we have more energy and are in a lighter mood. This is also quite normal.

However, when checking our mood becomes a trigger for feeling down for a prolonged period and, in the worst case, for depression, it is due to how much we focus on our mood. Do you often think that your mood is so bad that you need a day on the sofa? Do you notice yourself being a bit sad or a little happier several times a day? Do you ask yourself:

- How am I doing today?

- Am I sadder than usual?

- Why am I feeling like that?

If you often feel down, or if you have or have had depression, you probably focus more on your mood than is wise. Monitoring thoughts and feelings in the hope of catching any first symptoms of depression is a common strategy. Perhaps you think that if you are feeling a period of sadness coming on, you can take the right measures by taking care of yourself and slowing the pace so it doesn't develop. It's a tempting strategy, but it takes time and mental energy away from other experiences and chores in everyday life and can, therefore, result in a setback, where you risk stress and symptoms of depression in the aftermath.

People who pay close attention to their emotional life inevitably feel any small irregularity. In order to help clarify this monitoring behaviour for my clients, I ask them, for example, how often they monitor their mood, or if they just leave their mood alone without analysing it. Our normal mood is dynamic and alternates from day to day. Sometimes, we wake up in an inexplicably worse mood than the day before. Therefore, the best thing we can do when we feel sad is to do as little as possible with the sad thoughts and instead let our emotions regulate themselves. Look at emotional life like breathing: it regulates itself best when we don't always think about it and try to breathe in a certain way.

Strategy no. 4:
INAPPROPRIATE COPING BEHAVIOUR

The fourth strategy that can lead to setbacks is inappropriate coping behaviour. The term includes all those things we do to dull unpleasant thoughts and feelings. These inappropriate strategies are very common, but just like excessive rumination, worry and excessive monitoring behaviour, they can bite back in the form of sadder thoughts, feeling even more down and symptoms of depression. For people with depression, inappropriate coping mechanisms can worsen the condition. Let me illustrate this with some examples.

1. **We avoid or suppress certain thoughts and feelings.**

   It is a firm and widely accepted belief that the source of depression is having many negative thoughts. In light of this, it makes sense to try to avoid or escape from negative thoughts. However, thoughts don't work like this, and the more we focus on avoiding them, the more we can be sure they will occupy our consciousness.

2. **We try to change the negative thoughts into more positive or realistic thoughts.**

   A tempting approach can be to try to think more carefully or positively about yourself: 'You're doing your best. It'll all be ok,' we affirm again and again. The strategy is energy-intensive and involves more thinking. Your problem is not your negative thoughts but first and foremost too much thinking.

3. **We become angry with ourselves for thinking or feeling a certain way.**

Some of us get angry with ourselves when we lack energy or when we spend yet another evening on the sofa watching television. We may also become angry and judge ourselves if, for example, we feel we have lost the love of those we care for or if we no longer enjoy activities we usually find fun and exciting, such as playing sports, visiting museums and having dinner with friends. When experiences and relationships that usually bring happiness no longer feel enjoyable, we understandably become both sad and frustrated. When we get angry with ourselves on top of these feelings, it gives rise to new ruminations: 'Why am I so ugly? Why can't I get myself together? What am I doing wrong that I don't feel happy?' But this strategy of blaming ourselves for our lethargy and lack of feelings doesn't contribute to more positive feelings – quite the opposite. It is equivalent to ruminating about ruminations and, as a result, we end up ruminating even more. If our strategy is to force ourselves to think and feel differently, then all we are doing is replacing our first ruminations with new ones – and we back at square one. It is impossible to think yourself to fewer ruminations.

4. We sleep or rest more than usual.

Most of us experience having less energy when we are depressed or sad. On such days or during such periods we therefore want to rest more or sleep for longer. It's nice to go to bed early or take a nap in the middle of the day if you're feeling a little down. It's both normal and fine to give yourself a little extra care some days. But if this habit takes over, it's an inappropriate coping mechanism that can lead you to feeling even more down and to symptoms of depression. We don't become happier and more energised by lying on the sofa for hours every day. For people with depressive symptoms or depression itself, fatigue, lethargy and doing the bare minimum often go hand-in-hand. It can be tempting to try to rest or sleep so as to increase our energy. The problem with this strategy is that it leads to the opposite: if we rest a lot and sleep more than seven to nine hours a day, we risk feeling even more tired, unhappy and sad.

5. We dull our feelings with drugs or alcohol.

After a long, hectic day it may be nice to relax with a glass of wine at dinner or perhaps a beer with colleagues after work. It's not uncommon for a couple of glasses in the evening to feel soothing during stressful periods, such as during a highly pressured period at work or when coping with family illness or marital problems. However, it is obvious that the soothing effect is only temporary. Alcohol can – like marijuana and other intoxicating substances – make us feel free and happy, but when you come down from the high, the ruminations return at full force. Alcohol and drugs actually only cause more negative thoughts and ruminations because the fear of being unable to keep away from the red wine or the joint creates new negative thoughts, ones that can lead us into a vicious spiral that feels uncontrollable. Another negative consequence is that the alcohol keeps us from discovering our ability to control our ruminations. We hand over control to alcohol and the outside world instead.

Some people cultivate fantasies about alcohol and other intoxicating substances. This is so-called 'desire thinking', which often replaces the sad or angry ruminations – although only temporarily. It is quite normal to get a sudden urge for an ice-cold beer. But to fantasise for hours a day about drinking ice cold beer is not good. It will increase the likelihood of actually going out and drinking a number of beers. The extent of the desire thinking is crucial to whether or not we end up battling, for example, eating problems or alcoholism, alongside experiencing depressive thoughts.

6. We avoid social situations, hobbies or work.

When we're in high spirits, well and full of energy, many of us want to be with friends and family, to arrange gatherings and parties, and to participate in events at work, with clubs and at the children's school. When we are feeling down, we are more likely to withdraw from other people, decline to attend social activities and stop partaking in our hobbies. It is, of course, completely fine to reduce your number of social gatherings for a while, but the strategy may be inappropriate if it takes over. Then it equates to peeing in your trousers to keep warm – not a good long-term strategy for warmth or comfort! At first, it seems easier not to have to go to a friend's birthday party or a family event at your aunt and uncle's, but that sense of relief doesn't last. Unfortunately, by avoiding social interactions, you only increase the amount of time you spend on rumination. Because now you can also contemplate whether not going to the party was the right thing to do. And about what the others at the party must think: whether they will be upset and talk about how you always decline invitations. Social isolation leads to more ruminations which, in turn, can lead to symptoms of depression.

One reason for avoiding social gatherings can be to escape new negative thoughts and ruminations that result from seeing the happiness of others. It can be difficult to handle thoughts such as: 'Everyone else is so happy. They are better than me. My life has no meaning, and others have goals and plans for the future.' Evasive manoeuvres are always inappropriate. They only provide relief in the short term. In the long run, they maintain symptoms of depression or depression itself. When we avoid life, we don't experience that we can actually handle the challenges it brings. If we isolate ourselves from the world, we miss out on potentially good experiences, encounters and events that might lighten our mood. And if we end up having to take a leave of absence from work, we create even better conditions for spending time ruminating, worrying and keeping an eye on our mood.

7. We avoid thinking about and planning for the future.

If we lack energy and are afraid of things going badly, we may try to get rid of the dark thoughts by completely refraining from thinking about and planning for the future. Instead of solving the problems we face, we avoid thinking about them. We stick our heads in the sand like an ostrich and are fine as long as we don't think about reality. But when we choose to look the other way for a long time, the problems grow bigger and bigger, and we end up feeling like we need to focus on them even more, spending increasing amounts of time thinking about them.

I'd like to illustrate the elements of CAS strategies using the case of a female client who came to my clinic because she was unable to put her foot down with her grown son who had major mental and social difficulties. He would often ring his mother asking for money, and she would say yes, despite knowing that it wasn't helping her son manage things for himself in the long run. She ruminated for several hours a day about the consequences of giving him money, and she also ruminated about her own lack of strength to say no to him. Both subjects led to new thoughts, and she felt caught in a vicious circle, which she felt she had no control over (ruminations). When, after a while, she developed sleeping problems, she also began to worry about the consequences of the lack of sleep (worry). She also began to keep an eye on her son by calling and writing to him, and she downloaded an app to monitor how much sleep she was getting (monitoring behaviour). When the app told her that she hadn't been sleeping properly, she worried more. Her mood became so low that she began to withdraw from social arrangements (inappropriate coping mechanism).

The many ruminations, worries, sleep monitoring and avoidance of social situations meant that the woman developed symptoms of depression and felt sad, lethargic and unhappy.

Contemplations like this client's are quite normal: her son was in difficulty, which made her unhappy, and she wondered what to do about it. The problem was that her ruminations filled her waking hours. On days when she gave in to her son's wish and lent him money, she ruminated about the great disservice she was doing both him and herself, and on days when she managed to put her foot down, she ruminated about not supporting her son.

When the woman started metacognitive therapy and discovered that her primary problem was not struggling to put her foot down but ruminating too much over it, she learned to help herself. She decided that, regardless of whether or not she gave in to her son's badgering for money, she had to minimise her ruminations. She ruminated for an hour a day at most and that limitation gave her more energy and reduced her symptoms. After a few weeks, she found it easier to say no to her son's requests because she was no longer struggling with sadness and low self-esteem as a mother.

METACOGNITIVE BELIEFS MAINTAIN OUR CAS

For people who suffer from feeling down, from symptoms of depression or from depression itself, the four strategies that constitute CAS – ruminations, worries, monitoring behaviour and inappropriate coping mechanisms – will be immediately noticeable. Some of the strategies may have a positive and calming effect in the short term. For example, it may seem like a productive response to ruminate thoroughly over things once in a while because the immediate effect can be gaining a sense of overview. Sharing your worries with a good friend can give instant peace of mind. It may also be a relief to wake up one morning and observe a slight improvement in your mood after a mood check. And it can also be relaxing to avoid social gatherings that could trigger negative thoughts and feelings. But the effects of these strategies are short-lived; they largely only help to increase the darkness of depression.

It is a widespread perception among people who feel down for prolonged periods or suffer from depression that they have to take extra care of themselves, that they must do everything they can to catch the warning signs of depression in time. But this strategy also results in setbacks. Once you create an exaggerated focus on your inner life, you notice every little dip in your mood, and it can give rise to new self-fulfilling ruminations: 'Why am I in a bad mood? Oh no, am I on my way into depression again?'

As mentioned, metacognitive therapy is not about completely avoiding ruminations and worries; rather it's about limiting the time spent on them and directing our focus outwards instead. This enables us to be happy, to minimise or get rid of the symptoms of depression and – if we suffer from recurrent depression – to avoid relapses.

In order to be able to change the mechanisms that maintain depression, we need to find out what leads to CAS. This is where it becomes a little complicated, because the answer is found in our so-called *metacognitive beliefs*, those beliefs and assumptions in our internal control system which govern our behaviour (the metacognitive beliefs level of the S-REF model on page 11). As we previously touched upon, these beliefs and assumptions are concerned with what we believe or know about our thoughts and thought processes.

Adrian Wells and his colleagues determined through their research that when a person ruminates more than others, it is primarily due to one or more of the following five metacognitive beliefs. Each belief maintains our tendency to ruminate and worry too much:

A. I am not aware of my ruminations (lack of awareness).

A metacognitive belief is about awareness. In order to control our ruminations, it is vital that we notice when we are ruminating ourselves into a black hole. Many people

– particularly those who are sad, feel down or suffer from symptoms of depression – ruminate without noticing it. Only when they awake from their stream of thought do they notice that they have spent hours in their own world, drawn to their thoughts like a magnet, without being conscious of life or the world around them.

B. My rumination is uncontrollable (without control).

We may notice our ruminations but feel that we don't have control over them. We can't control our thoughts (they are uncontrollable and come from the lower level of the S-REF model), but we can control and limit the time we spend ruminating on them. In order to limit our ruminations, it is crucial that we fundamentally believe that this is possible. And that we try to limit the time spent ruminating by using the right techniques.

C. I can't act without motivation (passivity).

Another common misconception is that you can only act – for example, get out of bed or go for a walk – if you are motivated and in the right mindset. We all know the feeling of having an enormous urge to stay under the warm covers on a grey Monday morning in January. Some people are convinced that they can act even when they feel such urges: that despite absolutely not wanting to, they can crawl out of bed and get to work. Others wait for motivational thoughts to get them out from under the duvet and out the door. Our belief that we can act without desire determines whether or not we can stick to a fixed schedule or plan of action regardless of our thoughts and mood.

D. If I ruminate, I can find solutions and answers (usefulness).

The fourth metacognitive belief that determines how much we ruminate is the view that we can benefit from rumination – or not. If we believe that our ruminations can lead us to answers and solutions to our problems, it makes sense for us to spend hours every day on them. Many of the people who come to my clinic are convinced that their ruminations make them, for example, creative or smarter. Others are convinced that thoughts and feelings need to be processed thoroughly so as to feel less burdening, for example, through hour-long conversations. As a result, they are ambivalent when I explain to them that the way out of depression is to limit rumination.

E. Depression is a biological disease that I can't influence (biology).

The fifth metacognitive belief is based on the widespread perception that depression is a biological or genetic disease. Some believe that they have a brain defect, that they lack the neurotransmitter serotonin, that they suffer from uniquely negative thoughts, that they are particularly sensitive or that their emotional life is richer than others'. When you are convinced that the disease is caused by an internal defect, or is a distinctive feature of who you are, you fail to recognise that you are healthy and have an influence on your condition. It is crucial that in your attempt to ruminate less, you don't blame the depression on your brain or view it as a distinctive genetic feature.

RE-ESTABLISHING CONTROL

Some clients are convinced that they have no control over their ruminations when they start metacognitive therapy. Rather they believe that the thoughts just appear, attracting attention to themselves, and that they can't control the time they spend ruminating. Others have so often heard that depression is caused by a flaw in the brain that they are quite surprised to hear that nothing is wrong with their brain function but with their strategies.

If this sounds like you, I would encourage you to read on and to give metacognitive therapy a chance. Because you *have* an influence. You *can* get help to avoid symptoms of depression and in many cases to completely overcome depression. During a course of metacognitive therapy, you would follow – just like the four people you'll meet in this book – five metacognitive steps. You would learn to:

1. Become aware of your trigger thoughts and ruminations so that you can intervene in time.

2. Believe that you have control over your ruminations so that you can limit them.

3. Let go of the belief that ruminations lead to solutions to your problems, whether they be work-related, personal or even stemming from worry about becoming depressed or from fear of not being able to get past depression.

4. Stick to a plan of action regardless of your mood and to believe that you are able to do things in your everyday life that you don't really want to.

5. Believe that your thoughts and feelings are normal and harmless and that you are not a genetic victim of depression.

During a course of metacognitive therapy, clients are guided in how to overcome the beliefs that stand in their way. Clients learn to curtail their ruminations and to see that they themselves can play an important role in preventing and overcoming feeling down and depressed.

Naturally, a course of metacognitive therapy will not prevent feelings of sadness when life is painful. Grief, longing and pain are feelings that everyone experiences. But through therapy, you can discover that you don't have to ruminate so much and can learn to take control.

Chapter 2

BECOME AWARE OF TRIGGER THOUGHTS AND RUMINATIONS

Rumination, worry, monitoring behaviour and inappropriate coping mechanisms – these may seem like a lot of new ideas to grasp and an ever-harder challenge to overcome them. How can we break free from old habits? Is it even possible? I cannot promise that it will be easy or very quick. But I want to assure you that *it can be done*. Over the next four chapters I will take you step by step on a metacognitive journey. This chapter will show how we can become more aware of the trigger thoughts that can set off ruminations. Then in Chapter 3 we will see how to take control of ruminations by using metacognitive therapy. Chapter 4 describes the dilemmas we may encounter along the way to establishing new beliefs. And Chapter 5 will describe how to maintain these strategies and plans and bring our dreams to life.

Our brains bombard us with thoughts – hour after hour, night and day. Like other organs in the body our brains do this completely automatically and continuously. Our hearts beat, our stomachs digest and our brains create endless thoughts and images. The content of this input from the brain is a mix of pretty much everything we have paid attention to and remembered.

Try asking yourself these questions:

- How many thoughts did I have yesterday?

- Where are these thoughts now?

It is impossible to answer. Nobody can count their thoughts individually. Thoughts have their own lives. They do not necessarily begin and end clearly but interact and intersect with one another, and thus do not allow themselves to be accounted for. Researchers exploring the number of thoughts produced by the human brain estimate that people have between 30,000 and 70,000 thoughts a day. But this estimate doesn't tell us much about where those thoughts go, and how we prioritise which thoughts to focus on and which to let go. That process is not so simple.

We can compare our thoughts to trains at a busy railway station with a large number of platforms. Intercity trains, local stopping services and perhaps also underground or metro trains arrive into and depart from the station. There are departures all the time to hundreds of different destinations. Each train represents a thought or sequence of thoughts.

Let us take as an example the thought: 'What should I make for dinner?' Such a thought can, so to speak, arrive at the mental platform while we are doing something else – for instance, reading a book or checking emails on our phone. We may catch the thought and then notice that several others join onto it: 'What have I got in the fridge? Perhaps I should buy a bag of potatoes and some broccoli on the way home.' Or maybe we dismiss the thought, letting the train pass us by, since we suddenly remember that our neighbour has invited us over for dinner. Maybe we just let the thought about the evening meal be – sitting at the platform until we're ready to catch it – and turn our attention back to the book or phone, fully engaged with the content.

The question is whether we are conscious of our choice to engage with the thought or not. What happens to the thought that we do not expend energy on? The answer is that if we don't seize upon the thought, it will either remain on the platform for later or simply pass us by.

The majority of the 30,000–70,000 thoughts that our brain produces every day are completely insignificant to us. But some will affect us emotionally. These thoughts have some significance to us and, for one reason or another, demand our attention. In metacognitive therapy we call these 'trigger thoughts'. They are thoughts which can set a strong reaction in motion.

Trigger thoughts can trigger us in positive ways: for example, we are happy thinking about going on holiday with the whole family to a sunny Greek island, or about cosy evenings filled with warmth and moonlight.

They can, however, also trigger us in negative ways and can run the risk of leading us into a web of extensive ruminations: for example, thinking about being fired from a job, a conflict in the workplace, or family problems. When life is difficult it is natural to have more trigger thoughts than when life is full of happiness. These thoughts can be the first steps towards depressive symptoms, and therefore it is vital that we discover our trigger thoughts in time. This way we can let them be before they start to run away with us.

But how do we know which of the thousands of thoughts we have are trigger thoughts? It can be hard to sort through them all. A trigger thought is the first thought in a sequence of associations which has not yet turned into long-term rumination, like a train to which more and more carriages are joined, one after another. The train gets heavier and heavier and slower and slower, and finally it can no longer propel itself up even the slightest hill. The same applies to our trigger thoughts. The more time we spend on these thoughts the heavier they make us feel.

WE CHOOSE OUR DESTINATION OURSELVES

Learning to change our internal monitoring system begins with us learning to identify our trigger thoughts and working out whether or not to board the trigger thought train or to remain on the platform and let the train leave without us on board.

Thoughts come in different forms. There is no shortage of ones that create problems. Some – such as the one about the evening meal – are neutral. When at 10am I think, 'What should I make for dinner?', I can probably quite quickly decide whether to make cauliflower cheese or chicken curry, or to let the thought lie until I go to the supermarket in the afternoon.

Other thoughts might seem more difficult to observe passively and let go. A thought like 'Why do I feel so sad all the time?' can lead to ruminations: 'Colleagues definitely don't like me. I make far too many mistakes at work. I am a boring woman to be married to. I wonder if my husband is unhappy in our marriage.' What is crucial is whether I try to address the thought or just let it be. Although the 'Why do I feel so sad all the time?' thought pulls up in front of me and opens its doors, *I don't have to board it*. If I jump onto the train – begin to analyse the thought – and it triggers several other thoughts, then I am adding on a large number of carriages, slowing the train down and making it as heavy as my mood.

Or, instead of trains, we might picture our thoughts as the many small plates on a conveyor belt in a sushi restaurant. Plates of sushi (thoughts) pass by one after the other. You can choose to reach for them or let them pass by. If you don't take the fish rolls, they will stay on the belt and after a moment go around the corner and disappear out of sight. Even if they come back round a little later, you still don't have to take them. The same applies to a thought such as 'I am sad.' You can pick it up or you can let it go.

Even a relatively neutral thought like 'What shall I do at the weekend?' can be a trigger thought. Other thoughts can quickly couple with it: 'I have no plans. Should I ask someone if they want to do something? What if nobody is free, or if they just say yes to be polite? I'm so dull, lazy and boring the way I am at the moment. I don't contribute anything at all to conversations. So, what should I do at the weekend? Will I just be bored? My life is boring.' One thought leads to another, and after one hour of ruminating the thought which remains could very well be: 'My life is empty, and I am so boring that nobody would get anything out of being with me. Everything is hopeless. I am a total fiasco.'

This example shows how a completely neutral thought can lead to existential ruminations. And how these existential speculations can result in depressive conclusions if we circle round them for hours every day.

▶ **This is what I do in my clinic:**

HOW TO BECOME AWARE OF THE EXTENT OF RUMINATION

When people come to my clinic for help with beating depression, I initiate treatment by talking about cognitive attentional syndrome (CAS). I guide the person towards an understanding of what their CAS looks like, so that they rediscover control over the elements of CAS which figure most prominently for them. Not all people engage in the same level of rumination, worry, monitoring behaviour and inappropriate coping mechanisms. Therefore, it is beneficial for the therapy that the client and I work together to evaluate this level and to get as accurate an answer as possible.

For many people, evaluating the extent of their own rumination and mood-monitoring behaviour can seem like a difficult task. But it can be done, and we can build a relatively accurate picture by using this simple method.

I ask the client to rank, on a scale of zero to 100, how much they have ruminated about, worked on, or tried to avoid or suppress their thoughts and feelings in the past week.

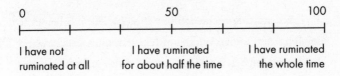

A woman came to my clinic who had discovered that her husband had been unfaithful to her. Now most of her days were filled with ruminating about their relationship. Her husband was distraught, apologetic and adamant that he had no desire for any woman other than his wife and that being unfaithful had been a terrible mistake. The couple agreed to stay together, but the woman found it hard to trust her husband again, and trigger thoughts were going round and round her head: 'Is he being completely honest when he says he wants to stay with me? Why was he unfaithful?'

The woman began to check her husband's phone and Facebook page in the hope of reassuring herself when she did not find any sign of new affairs. Her strategy belongs to the category of inappropriate coping mechanisms because it did not reassure her.

She ruminated for six to eight hours a day over thoughts like: 'Is there something wrong with me? Am I a bad wife? Am I too grumpy?' She had problems sleeping, lacked energy and became tired and depressed.

My client was aware that she was ruminating. But she was not aware that ruminating reinforced the sad thoughts. On the contrary, she was convinced that it would help her find answers and stop her feeling sad and jealous.

Since starting metacognitive therapy, she has begun to develop a new understanding of her symptoms. She now sees that her attempt to find solutions and answers just prolonged the problem. The woman wanted first and foremost to benefit from this therapy and to improve her mood. Once she had learned to limit rumination, the depressive symptoms lessened and she experienced more energy and increased self-esteem.

Later in the book we will encounter the stories of Natacha, Mette, Leif and Berit, who shared this client's problem: it was not that they had too many thoughts, nor that they had negative thoughts. The problem was that they tore themselves to pieces with these thoughts. They dwelled upon them, chewed them over, analysed them, reflected and ruminated upon them, and overthought to such a degree that it dominated their everyday life and made them depressed.

WE RUMINATE ABOUT DIFFERENT THINGS AS WE GO THROUGH LIFE.

Children and young people typically ruminate about their mothers' and fathers' welfare: Why is mum so upset about that? What would happen if my parents were to split up?

Teenagers typically speculate about their bodies, sex, boyfriends or girlfriends, and the future: Are others in my class ahead of me? Why am I the only virgin on the football team? Why did I get such a bad mark in that last piece of work? Will I pass my exams?

Adult life offers many challenges and topics to ruminate about – finances, career, colleagues and relationship problems can take up a lot of our headspace and lead to stress and symptoms of depression: Why don't I feel the same way about my partner as I used to? Have I chosen the right job?

TRIGGER THOUGHTS ARE PERSONAL

Many different thoughts can trigger us. Person A may tear themselves apart with guilt-riddled trigger thoughts to which Person B would not react at all. Person B meanwhile may have anxiety-driven trigger thoughts which have never crossed Person A's mind. It is also very normal to experience trigger thoughts that change over time. This is because trigger thoughts reflect our most intense feelings. Depending on which thoughts dominate, this can range from extreme guilt, stress or anxiety to great irritation and mania.

If someone is afraid of becoming depressed, or if they tend to feel down and sad, becoming aware of which types of thought trigger them can be a great help.

Sad trigger thoughts:

'Why am I so sad? Why don't I feel anything anymore? Why do I get depressed? Was it the divorce, my father's death or the abortion?'

Sad trigger thoughts typically have negative content, and ruminations about these thoughts reinforce a bad, low mood. This type of trigger thought can be very dangerous and lead to many depressive ruminations.

Angry trigger thoughts:

'Why does nobody understand me? Why are the local authority, my doctor and my spouse so indifferent? People are idiots and egoists. They deserve to be punished.'

Angry trigger thoughts are typically aggressive in content, with fantasies about how to take revenge on and punish other people.

Anxious trigger thoughts:

'What happens if I never get any better? What if my child inherits my sensitivity? What if I go bankrupt and have to move out of my house?'

Anxious trigger thoughts typically begin with 'What if …' and can end in an anxiety attack and an excessive focus on avoiding situations and places.

Guilt-laden trigger thoughts:

'I should pull myself together. I should be a better, more present mother.'

Guilt-laden trigger thoughts typically begin with 'I should …'. They can end with low self-esteem, an inability or lack of motivation to take the initiative in activities or to be in touch with people to make arrangements, and avoidance of certain situations – in the same way as is often the case with people who suffer from anxious trigger thoughts.

Hopeless trigger thoughts:

'My life is meaningless. It will never get better. Why should I carry on living and be a burden to my family?'

Many hopeless trigger thoughts lead to a person becoming passive and inactive, unable to do anything. In the worst-case scenario, hopeless trigger thoughts can lead to suicidal thoughts and, in rare cases, to suicide attempts.

Suicide-related trigger thoughts:

'How can I end it all? Nobody will miss me. I wish I were dead.'

After many drawn-out ruminations, it is not unusual for suicidal thoughts to intrude. Suicide-related trigger thoughts can lead to actually planning how to commit suicide. Some people may even write suicide notes. The more concrete the ruminations are, the more life-threatening they are, because many suicide ruminations increase the risk of actually enacting the thought in real life.

For some depressed people, suicidal thoughts can feel comforting because they might give them the feeling that there is a way out of depression. Ruminations about suicide can therefore replace difficult negative ruminations about being depressed.

I should like to emphasise that if you are having suicidal thoughts, immediately seek advice from your doctor or psychologist. You cannot heal yourself with inspiration from this book alone.

Once we have identified our trigger thoughts, the next step is to find out how much time we spend ruminating each day. The four clients whose stories we follow in this book used to spend between six hours and most of the day ruminating before they started metacognitive therapy.

TRIGGER THOUGHTS CAN BE INCARNATE TRUTHS

Some people will feel provoked that I refer to 'trigger thoughts'. They might feel that the term indicates the thought is trivial and unimportant. Mette, whom you will meet on page 96, felt hampered by this designation. She had been bullied by two former colleagues and was in a terrible state when she came to me for therapy. She viewed 'trigger thought' as condescending, as though the thoughts were something that she should be able to just brush aside. But it is not meant like this. Trigger thoughts can represent very real concerns, such as Mette's fear of social gatherings after years of bullying. You will also meet Leif (page 117), who had a great and real fear of dying, and Natacha (page 59), who tells us about her fear of failure. Trigger thoughts can be factual truths, such as you have been fired, been abandoned, been ill or gone bankrupt. Because the thoughts are based in truth, you might believe that you *should* continue to dwell on these thoughts.

But the truth is that even if the ruminations are rooted in reality, it does not help to ruminate. It does not lessen the insecurity associated with being fired, the sorrow of having been left behind, the pain of illness, or the outrage of being summoned to bankruptcy court. Ruminations do not contribute to happiness, self-esteem and insight – let alone a new job, better health or more secure finances. Instead they keep thoughts alive, such as whether we are unlovable, or whether nobody will want to employ us again. These are thoughts which can make anyone who ruminates on them depressed.

We can easily be knowledgeable about things which make us uncomfortable without expending much energy dwelling on that knowledge. When I look at all the truths in my life, I find that I *know* an incredible amount that I don't go around expending a lot of energy on. This is knowledge which I just can just leave to look after itself.

I know that I like Thai food with a lot of chili and that I cannot stand strong liver. I also sometimes know long before an election who I am going to vote for and who I am not going to vote for. I know which day of the week it is. I know which bus I have to take to town. But these truths don't mean much to me. We have a whole mass of knowledge about unpleasant things which don't fill our minds for many hours a day. But when those unpleasant things are personal, the thoughts can linger longer. We have all experienced feeling like losers. Sometimes I know that I am good enough, other times that I have behaved stupidly. But why ruminate about it when ruminating can contribute to further sadness? Even if I am completely convinced that it is true that I am a loser, the feeling will disappear into itself again, and self-esteem will return if I avoid reinforcing this conviction. The point is that unpleasant truths don't have to fill our minds any more than the factual ones.

It is vital to take control and decide how much time, energy and attention we want to give to rumination. When we decide to scale down the time spent, we will experience that, even under difficult living circumstances, we can control our ruminations and thus avoid having to contend with yet another problem: depression.

The journey from the first trigger thought to depression is long and involves many ruminations. A lot of my clients tear themselves apart with ruminations to such a degree that they spend many hours a day on it. Such a long rumination period gives rise to depressive symptoms, such as feeling despondent, hopeless and stagnant and often having sleep problems too. I am not detailing these sad consequences to discourage you but to emphasise the importance of knowing your trigger thoughts. It's not until you are on first name terms with them that you will recognise them as you go through life and choose what you want to do with them.

The illustration below – Adrian Wells' metacognitive model – shows the path from trigger thoughts to depression. Please note, however, that there is no direct arrow between trigger thoughts and depression. It is not the negative trigger thoughts that give us symptoms. These only last a few seconds. It is the many hours we spend dealing with and processing the trigger thoughts that result in depressive symptoms.

We can therefore easily have negative thoughts and convictions without becoming depressed. We probably all know someone who has real financial, health or emotional difficulties and who therefore has negative thoughts but has not become depressed.

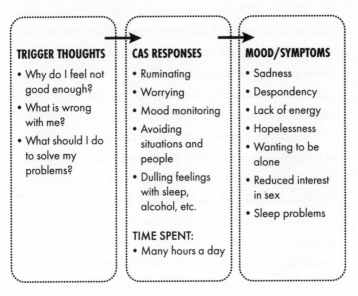

TRIGGER THOUGHTS
- Why do I feel not good enough?
- What is wrong with me?
- What should I do to solve my problems?

CAS RESPONSES
- Ruminating
- Worrying
- Mood monitoring
- Avoiding situations and people
- Dulling feelings with sleep, alcohol, etc.

TIME SPENT:
- Many hours a day

MOOD/SYMPTOMS
- Sadness
- Despondency
- Lack of energy
- Hopelessness
- Wanting to be alone
- Reduced interest in sex
- Sleep problems

SOURCE: AMC model from Wells (2009)

Many of us have experienced this ourselves. We can easily think, 'Why am I not good enough?', without this thought in itself leading to depression.

The causes of depression can, as mentioned, be found in our negative strategies for dealing with trigger thoughts, as you can see in the illustration above. The illustration shows how trigger thoughts, which are dealt with long-term with CAS (cognitive attentional syndrome) responses, can have an effect on your mood and cause symptoms. If a trigger thought hits me in the morning, and I jump onto the thought train and begin to process and analyse it for many hours, I will very probably be in a bad mood in the afternoon. A trigger thought such as: 'What is the meaning of my life?' can easily take us to: 'It is completely meaningless!' The time we use to speculate about internal and external events in our life is decisive in determining whether we simply experience a natural feeling of distress and sadness, or whether we develop clinical depression.

Let me repeat: it is not the negative thoughts in themselves that cause depression. So, we don't have to turn the negative thoughts into positive ones. We just have to let them be.

When clients come to me for therapy, I first show them a blank copy of the table (shown on the opposite page) that we can fill in with their own trigger thoughts, responses and resulting symptoms. I ask about which thoughts directly affect them and set their rumination in motion. At various points I also show them the completed form (page 73), because it can be hard to see their own trigger thoughts and which strategies they currently use clearly. I ask the client to tell me about the last time they felt down or in a bad mood and ask: 'What was the first thought that pushed you into this situation?' That is their trigger thought.

Next I ask what they did with the thought: 'Did you leave it be or did you do something with it?' Most clients say they dealt with the thought. I ask how much time they spend every day ruminating about their trigger thoughts, monitoring their mood, worrying and engaging in things that I would consider 'inappropriate coping mechanisms', such as avoiding situations they do not like, or numbing their feelings with alcohol. I note the time spent in the centre field of the table.

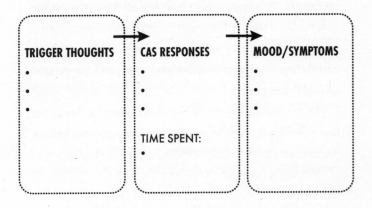

▶ **This is what I do in my clinic:**

TO BECOME AWARE OF TRIGGER THOUGHTS AND RUMINATION TIME

In clinic we start with discussions of thinking. That may sound a little abstract, but it is the first step to becoming aware of trigger thoughts and rumination.

For example, I ask the client: 'When do you ruminate? How long do you ruminate for?' And most importantly: 'Which trigger thoughts set off your ruminations?'

I ask my clients to try to become aware quickly of when they are ruminating so that they don't spend so much time doing it. This is not necessarily easy. Maybe the thoughts have filled the whole of the train journey home after work, or while preparing a meal, or during a TV programme which they may have really wanted to watch but which afterwards they cannot remember much about. The more time is spent — daily rumination time — the greater the risk of developing symptoms of depression.

NATACHA

'I became good at leaving thoughts be and shifting my focus.'

When my doctor recommended metacognitive group therapy to me, I was upset about it. I didn't have the strength to talk about all my problems and listen to other people's bad experiences.

I had told my doctor all about what I had been through when I was at school, all about my difficult choices concerning education and about my feelings. I had told the psychiatrist the same things. I didn't feel I could manage to talk about it all again. I knew I would get upset about it and be completely drained of energy afterwards. So, it was gruelling for me to come to group therapy for the first time. But when I was sat there with the others, I realised that it really made no difference what particular baggage each of us had brought with us. It was liberating and showed me a whole new way of thinking. Previously I had worked on structuring my thoughts and thinking logically or positively with the psychologist. It was a relief to learn that you yourself can control how much energy you expend on thoughts. You cannot control your thoughts, but you can control whether you pay attention to them. This meant that, actually, I did not need to spend the whole time thinking.

In metacognitive therapy I learned that it makes no difference whether I am afraid of something real or something unreal. Instead, it is all about understanding that I myself can control how much attention and energy I wish to give to my experiences and life events. This way of thinking has completely changed my life. Regardless of what I have been through, I can control what I do with my thoughts.

A difficult time as a teenager

My symptoms started when I was a little girl. I was three, and my little sister a newborn baby when our mother became seriously ill. For a few years she was in and out of hospital and very often away from home. I began to suffer from severe stomach pains.

In school I did well academically, but it was not easy socially, and I often felt that the other girls were indifferent to me. My stomach problems started again when I was fourteen and, since the doctors could not find any physical cause for the symptoms, I was referred to a psychologist who diagnosed me with stress-related depression, arising from performance anxiety. Despite support from my father and from the psychologist, the depression has been a recurrent part of my life. It was at its worst in the first half of secondary school when I ended up with severe depression and anxiety.

I had cognitive therapy, which helped me a lot, but I stopped too early. I began to hallucinate and hear voices, so I began seeing a psychiatrist. But I stopped the treatment after just one consultation because I moved to a new town with my boyfriend to get away from everything. I did feel better – but this did not last.

I left high school and began a single subject Further Education course and got a job at a petrol station. After a short time, the deputy manager went off sick and I took over their work and discovered that it was a fantastically satisfying job that I was good at. After taking my Further Education exam, I started to study at teacher training college and managed to attend for half a year before I became pregnant. My boyfriend and I really wanted to be parents. But it stressed me out that the school was two hours from home, and I put a lot of energy into socialising because I always worried that the others didn't like me. I spoke to my doctor as I was so afraid that the stress would affect my pregnancy. Finally, I was signed off sick with stress.

It was when I was on maternity leave that the doctor recommended metacognitive therapy to me.

My biggest problem was always that I thought so much. I wrote lists, planned things, ruminated and speculated. I overthought absolutely everything, from 'I wonder if someone was angry about that thing I said yesterday' to 'Does my hair look OK at the moment?' to 'Do the people I sit with and talk to think I'm stupid?' to 'Am I ugly and fat?' If I didn't switch off by watching a film or TV series, which shut down the thoughts, then they would just keep running through my head all my waking hours. I also had problems relaxing and falling asleep. My brain was always ticking over.

Discovering meaning

I found my niche in the metacognitive group therapy. I have always been very interested in self-development and self-improvement. There, I learned that too much self-analysis can create problems.

The psychologist told participants who were sceptical about metacognitive therapy that there was no need to believe in this form of therapy. They just had to try it. This made a big impression on me. Participants were to drop everything else they were doing at the time, like thinking positively, meditating or practising mindfulness. And they discovered that metacognitive therapy worked.

I believe that we helped each other a lot in group therapy. We didn't spend two hours talking about the bad stuff, like I had done with other therapies. We each spent a minute and a half telling the group why we were there. This meant we progressed quickly. It was quite random, and it made absolutely no difference whether we had eating disorders, had suffered from PTSD, were depressed or something completely different. We discovered that all the others also had trigger thoughts – they just had different ones. It was great to hear what others had to share.

I found it hard to just let my thoughts be and to observe them passively. But I am good at switching focus from the inside to the outside. So, I learned to concentrate on what I was doing at the time. If I was washing up, for example, and started to ruminate, I would think about how the soap bubbles looked. This has given me strength in situations where previously I would have been taken hold of by a feeling, as I am now more easily able to let thoughts go, because I don't blame myself for being angry or upset about it. Now I just concentrate on something else.

One of the metaphors we heard during therapy has become a favourite of mine: 'You cannot walk away from a door you are trying to hold closed.' You cannot get away from a thought you are trying to hold on to. You have to let it be and move away from it. Go somewhere else. You should not try to suppress your thoughts or tell your feelings that they should not be there. You should just change focus and pay attention to something else.

Someone in my family has recently had a scan to look for a possible brain tumour. The doctors found something on the scan image, but they didn't know what it was, so they are doing another scan. Previously, I would have spent a great deal of time thinking about this and getting upset about it. But now when the worrying thoughts come, I can see that I can't do anything constructive with them. I have recognised that I can leave the thought be. I cannot investigate anything. I can only wait for the person concerned to tell me what is happening. So now, each time the thought comes up I just let it be. And carry on with my day.

For the first time since I was fourteen years old, I don't believe that I will suffer from depressive symptoms again. I have always thought, when I was doing well for a while, that it was only a matter of time before the symptoms came back. But this time I am sure that I won't get depression again. I have strategies to avoid it. Now I am really not concerned about it, which is so great. And it only took twelve hours of therapy for me to do this!

I am back in the market for work. I have been offered a job as deputy manager at a petrol station. And I am happy about this. I need to get out and do something now. I'm really just so happy to be doing things again – to start living again.

NATACHA'S PATH FROM TRIGGER THOUGHTS TO DEPRESSION

Natacha, who experienced a difficult childhood, developed depression and anxiety at an early age. The starting point for her trigger thoughts was seeking answers to things which had happened in the past, and fear of being a failure. The trigger thoughts typically arose in the evenings and on days when she should have been, or had just been, spending time with other people.

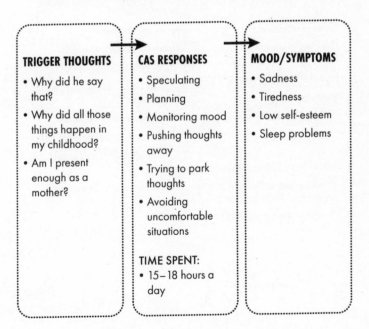

TRIGGER THOUGHTS
- Why did he say that?
- Why did all those things happen in my childhood?
- Am I present enough as a mother?

CAS RESPONSES
- Speculating
- Planning
- Monitoring mood
- Pushing thoughts away
- Trying to park thoughts
- Avoiding uncomfortable situations

TIME SPENT:
- 15–18 hours a day

MOOD/SYMPTOMS
- Sadness
- Tiredness
- Low self-esteem
- Sleep problems

NATACHA'S OLD STRATEGIES, WHICH CONTRIBUTED TO SYMPTOMS	NATACHA'S NEW STRATEGIES, WHICH OVERCAME THE SYMPTOMS
Thinking style:	**Thinking style:**
I analysed, worried and ruminated with other people.	I spend less time ruminating, and I have set aside a certain time of day for ruminating.
I tried to think logically and to plan.	I ruminate less with others.
	I spend less time trying to process negative thoughts.
Focus of attention:	**Focus of attention:**
I focussed a lot on my thoughts and feelings.	I focus on what is happening around me.
I focussed on planning and control.	
Behaviour:	**Behaviour:**
I avoided a lot of situations.	I make decisions more quickly.
	I do things regardless of the thoughts and feelings I have.

What I have learned about my thoughts:

I have learned that I control how much I ruminate and plan. It is me who decides how much attention thoughts get.

I don't find any solutions by ruminating.

CHAPTER 3

TAKE CONTROL —
YOU CAN DO IT

When you have become aware of your trigger thoughts and overthinking habits, you will learn that you have a choice because you are the one who controls how long you want to ruminate for about a trigger thought. I usually ask my clients when they come to their first metacognitive therapy session whether they have any idea as to how much they can control their ruminations. Most people shake their heads and say it is completely impossible to control their ruminations themselves.

I give them the below scale and ask them to mark their lack of control as a percentage. If their answer is 100 per cent, they are convinced that they cannot control their ruminations at all. If their answer is 0 per cent, they believe that they have full control over their ruminations. Most clients answer between 50 to 100 per cent: that their ruminations are, to a greater or lesser degree, out of their control.

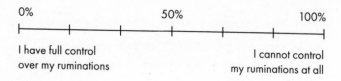

Some clients tell me that they have never been able to control their ruminations; others tell me that they have lost the feeling of control. Regardless of their convictions, I assure them that they have always had this control and can rediscover it. I use the therapy to guide them to rediscover their own feeling of control and to use the correct attention techniques to control their ruminations (we will learn about these techniques shortly).

When I introduce the therapy session in which the client is to rediscover this control, I typically set up the following scenario: Imagine that you are sitting at home dwelling on some of the problems you face in your life. Without you noticing it, your mood deteriorates. The problem you were ruminating about is replaced by another, and after a while your head becomes a jumble of dark thoughts. Suddenly there is a ring at the doorbell. It is a neighbour who has run out of milk and would like to borrow some from you. You invite her in and chat for a bit about the weather while you look for a carton of milk in the fridge. In just a short space of time your attention has moved to something other than the darkest thoughts about your hopeless situation. What has happened to your mood? It is quite likely that it has lifted a little.

Without realising it, you jumped off the thought train when your neighbour rang the doorbell and you responded to her. The interruption put your ruminating on pause – or maybe even shut it down completely. What would you say about your self-control? Who is controlling your ruminations? Was it the neighbour or you?

You could doubtless have continued to ruminate while the neighbour stood and chatted about the weather in your kitchen. So, the next time she comes round for a short visit to borrow something, try to see if you can absent yourself from the conversation for a while and consciously begin to ruminate over something other than what you are talking about. I am convinced that you will be able to do it. People are, in fact, good at thinking on command.

So, if you can force yourself to ruminate about your problems, then you can also force yourself to stop ruminating. It is tempting to conclude that it is only an interruption from outside that brings a ruminating session to a stop. But, thinking about it logically, you can see that the neighbour hardly has the power or the strength to control any mind other than her own. It is you yourself who decides to release the thoughts and focus your attention on talking with and listening to your neighbour. Therefore, it is absolutely you who is controlling your ruminations.

When my clients react to this conclusion with doubt and a frown, I ask them to think back to the last time they ruminated about problems or symptoms. I ask them how long they ruminated for. Five hours? Why not longer? I ask, what had prevented them from ruminating for ten or fifteen hours? It is not the scale of the problem that determines how long a person spends dwelling on it, but rather the person themselves who makes this evaluation.

As has been mentioned, we must overcome an over-thinking problem with thinking less, with ruminating less. Therefore, in metacognitive therapy we neither fight nor transform thoughts but just reduce rumination time. During the therapy I present three different methods of limiting rumination. All three require a change in your internal control system, so that old habits and convictions can be exchanged for new ones.

The first method is **A. DEFERRAL – SETTING A RUMINATION TIME**. This teaches clients to postpone their ruminations until a certain point in time, which they choose themselves. This is called *rumination time*. Before and after rumination time, I suggest that clients use methods B and C.

The second method teaches clients that they can **B. CONTROL THEIR ATTENTION** despite the trigger thoughts.

And with the third method they learn to **C. DETACH THEIR ATTENTION**, so that they just observe the trigger thoughts but avoid seizing upon them.

We have to make a choice when the trigger thoughts hit us, as illustrated in this model.

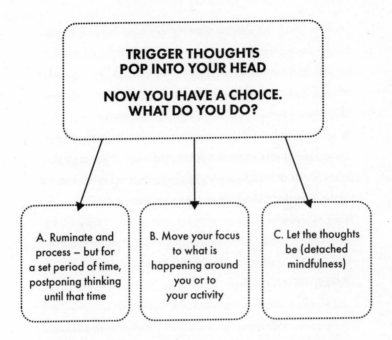

WE HAVE BEEN IN CONTROL THE WHOLE TIME

Let's go through the three methods one at a time. Before we begin with the first method, though, I want to emphasise that ruminating will first cause a dip in mood and increase the risk of symptoms of depression.

We all experience many problems and associated negative thoughts as we go through life. We have relationship problems, we experience defeats in school and at work, and we feel disappointed in family and friends. As a result, we ask ourselves questions like: Why did they leave me? Why didn't I get the job when I am qualified for it? Why don't our good friends want to go on holiday with us?

The negative thoughts often disappear all by themselves. After a while, real life intervenes and old experiences recede into the background. As a result, we may well believe that it is external factors (such as our neighbour showing up and chatting) which control our brain and what we think about. This is not the case. It is you alone who controls what happens in your brain. We ourselves have the power to decide which strategies to use for controlling our trigger thoughts. We can choose to let the negative thought train pass by – and naturally we will feel somewhat upset and sorry because of the thought – or we can board the train and let the thought carry us away. The longer we travel this route, the greater the risk that our feelings will increase.

We often use the word 'cultivate' to describe our excessive focus on an experience or a feeling. We choose to cultivate relationship problems after a fight or breakup by playing 'our song' on repeat for hours in an attempt to cry the sadness out of our system. We write diaries, talk to family and friends, and analyse by ourselves so as to 'offload' and gain some control over the sadness. But regardless of how much we try this, it usually has the opposite effect. We don't cry it out and we don't offload it; we are keeping these relationship problems alive and risk holding on to them until they result in depression.

Over the years that I have been practising metacognitive therapy, I have been asked many times: 'What should I do with all the thoughts? Should I push them away?' My answer is a resounding no. The problem does not lie in the fact that we have thoughts, and therefore the solution is not to repress them. Nor is it a good idea to numb them with alcohol, food, sex, drugs, self-harm, working long hours, or playing Words with Friends or Candy Crush on your phone. Distractions or diversionary tactics are tempting, but they ineffective. One thing you can be sure of is that the negative thoughts will return to the surface like a rubber duck from under the water as soon as we stop actively suppressing it.

Sometimes clients have told me that they ruminate on one particular thought simply to prevent themselves getting caught up in other more distressing ruminations. As long as our heads are filled with everyday worries about finances, shopping and cleaning, there is no room for worse trigger thoughts such as: 'Do I really love my husband?' or 'Am I worth anything?' I call this strategy the 'ruminating about ruminating strategy'. It goes without saying that it doesn't solve any problems. In fact, it is so stifling in the long term that it can lead to depression. The solution is instead to let the thought be. Or, as Wells often describes it: 'Do all you can to do nothing.' This means that the less you do with your thoughts, the better off you will be.

A. DEFERRAL – SETTING A RUMINATION TIME

It can feel enormously enticing – almost compelling – to let yourself get carried away by trigger thoughts when they crop up. 'Why did my boyfriend say that to me yesterday? What did he mean by it? Why do I have the feeling he is being unfaithful? How do I regain trust in other people?' Trigger thoughts can often be about real problems, challenges and difficulties, which do require thinking to solve. We need to think the whole thing through to gain some insight and to find the best answer. Perhaps our boss has real anger management issues that make us scared and uneasy. Maybe we have to choose an educational course or career path and apply within a deadline. Maybe our spouse has been unfaithful and left us disappointed and betrayed.

We have to address these challenges. We cannot stop the thoughts appearing altogether, nor can we control when they appear, but we can limit how much we think about them. Lengthy daily ruminations do not lead us to cleverer solutions than those we could have found in a shorter time. Our boss will not get any kinder just by us ruminating about them for ten hours a day. We will probably not come to a better course decision by continually mulling over the options. We can't turn back time to before our partner was unfaithful. These excessive ruminations rarely lead to any clarity, but often to greater confusion.

Instead, we should set aside a rumination time: a limited period of time in which we are allowed to analyse our problems. Many people choose to have their rumination time when they are sitting in the car on the way to work, when cooking a meal, or after the children have been put to bed. I always recommend that my clients choose a limited period of time that is convenient for both them and their family, and preferably not just before bedtime. A good time for many is from 8–9pm.

During the rumination time we can analyse our thoughts, feelings and problems, and take the necessary decisions. If we come across trigger thoughts before 8pm, then we should leave them be. We can of course acknowledge that they are there, but we should practise leaving them be. If we suddenly discover that we have let ourselves get carried away by a trigger thought and we are well into the swing of ruminating before 8pm, then we should decide to get off the thought train, let the thoughts be and avoid ruminating until 8pm. Some days we will probably discover that we have to force ourselves many times to get off the train. It takes time to change our control system.

Rumination time is not obligatory. If we don't feel up to ruminating on any given day, we should postpone the ruminations until the next day's rumination time.

If, on the other hand, we have so many ruminations that we feel we can't deal with them all in the set rumination time, we should not extend our period of rumination to try to deal with them. They must be left until the next day.

The metacognitive assistant will remember the important thoughts

'What if I forget what I am supposed to be ruminating about?' my clients often ask. Do we risk forgetting important thoughts during the day if we let them go now and avoid processing them until rumination time? Should we write a short note to ourselves about trigger thoughts so as to remember them? No, we shouldn't. I promise my clients that they should not be afraid of forgetting their trigger thoughts. If they are important enough – and a trigger thought by definition is one which concerns something emotionally significant – then our metacognitive assistant will do the work for us and bring the thoughts to our attention at rumination time.

Our metacognition is set up in such a smart way that we automatically remember the crucial challenges in our lives. If we have the thought 'Do I really want to do my job?' then we can easily remember it at 8pm. If we have forgotten it by 8pm, then it probably wasn't that important.

Gradually, you will find that you benefit more from having a limited rumination time, as well as experiencing more positive feelings, a better mood and a better night's sleep. Perhaps you will even discover that most problems solve themselves and only the most important require attention. I often find that clients overcome depression and despondency solely by limiting their ruminations.

How much may I ruminate?

Many of my clients ask how much they may ruminate if they want to avoid depression. It is difficult to set a limit. This depends to a great extent on how much we believe that we can stop ruminating. Our belief in our own control is crucial for how much distress we feel. However, if we are so convinced that we have control over our ruminations that we allow ourselves too much time to dwell because we can always stop when we decide to, our ruminations can easily run amok. I would generally recommend limiting rumination time to an hour a day at the most if you want to be free from depressive symptoms. That also applies even if you feel a great benefit from ruminations or have important decisions to make, such as: 'Which course should I take? Should I accept the job offer? Should we get married? Am I ready to have children?' Some mega-ruminators think of all the pros and cons for years in order to come to the 'best' decisions, when the same decisions could be made in less time and with less thought.

▶ This is what I do in my clinic:

TO SET A DAILY RUMINATION TIME

The one thing that people who come to me for metacognitive therapy have in common is that they ruminate for many hours a day. So, the therapy includes help in setting a rumination time. The target is a maximum of one hour a day, at a time when the client feels they could stick to this – for example, late in the afternoon or else in the evening.

Setting a rumination time means that if the trigger thoughts hit at 10am then you must say to yourself that you cannot analyse them until 8pm. If you find that you have boarded the thought train outside of the rumination time, then you must jump off again and postpone dealing with the thoughts until the rumination time.

Rumination times are not obligatory. That is to say, if rumination does not feel necessary or important, then it can be postponed until the next day.

B. CONTROLLING ATTENTION

I meet many clients who feel that they have lost control over their thinking. 'My thoughts run away with me,' they say. 'I can no longer control my thoughts like I could before.' The truth is that none of us can control our trains of thought, but we can all control whether we dwell on them or detach ourselves from them. When we choose to use this control in the right way – not trying to control the thoughts themselves but the way in which we deal with them – we will find that we have complete control.

Remember, it is not the thoughts in themselves that make us sad or depressed but ruminating too much about them. We may well feel that everything has gone to the dogs and think that life in general is a mess, without getting depressed about it. This is because we feel in control of our ruminations – even if we are not conscious of this feeling of control. People with a good experience of controlling their ruminations, and who use this control to limit ruminations, will not become depressed. Naturally they can have bad days and become despondent at times, but their conviction that they are in control and that they have a backstop means that they never ruminate for long enough to develop depression.

People who suffer from depression or who have previously had depression also have this backstop, which functions completely normally. Their ability to use self-control is as good as that of people who go through life without depression. They just don't believe it. This belief can be developed by becoming aware of trigger thoughts and ruminations, learning to defer the ruminations, and by shifting focus or detaching attention from the trigger thoughts.

Attention training is a central part of metacognitive therapy when used to combat depression. In the first therapy session with clients I introduce Adrian Wells' **attention training technique** (ATT). Training in this technique continues throughout the course of therapy.

Attention training is an awareness exercise, the purpose of which is to make us aware that we can change our focus, regardless of the thoughts and feelings within us or of what is happening around us. We decide whether we want to pay attention to our inner lives or to the wider world, or whether we want to share our attention between several elements at the same time. We also decide for how long we want to direct our attention to these different elements. The exercise helps us to regain control over our minds.

My clients who carry out attention training every day report that they feel psychologically better. They defer more, they get better at maintaining focus on what they want, and they experience fewer symptoms of depression. They also report that they can decide whether they want to mull over their thoughts many times a day, or whether they would prefer to shift their attention away from negative thoughts, feelings or images of themselves, or away from the outside world.

When I introduce attention training into the therapy, I tell my clients that the exercises should be done in a place where they can hear a range of different sounds at the same time.

They can keep their eyes open, and it is not necessary to have an 'empty mind'. When a negative thought, memory or feeling comes into their minds, they should observe it as though it were a sound: one sound among the many external noises they can hear. They should not try to push the thoughts away or distract themselves from them. Instead they should let the inner thoughts play; the thoughts may remain for a little while, change or disappear again. If they get distracted by them, the client should re-focus attention back on the other (external) sounds – one sound at a time.

If the client experiences anxious feelings or thoughts during attention training, they can be fully aware of the presence of these feelings or thoughts but should continue training without processing them.

I usually ask my clients where their attention is in relation to their inside and outside worlds *before* the initial training and again immediately *after* the initial training.

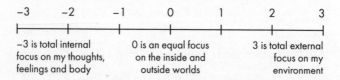

If the exercise is done correctly, I typically see a shift of at least two points towards the external environment. In contrast to mindfulness and meditation, which typically result in an increased internal focus, attention training increases external focus. It does not take long for attention training to have lasting effects, even for clients with symptoms of depression.

In order to achieve the best and quickest effect, I recommend that clients carry out the training twice a day. It does not have to be at the same time each day, but many people find it easier to keep to a fixed schedule. In addition, I emphasise that they should be patient with themselves and accept that sometimes they will succeed in this better than others.

▶ This is what I do in my clinic:

ATTENTION TRAINING WITH SOUNDS

During the metacognitive therapy course in clinic, we spend about ten minutes on attention training to close each session. The exercise helps clients to discover their ability to focus selectively, quickly change what they are paying attention to, and share their focus between multiple things. I introduce the training by presenting the client with a range of different sounds at the same time (at least three, but the more the better). Some find the exercise very difficult, and I recommend they begin with just two sounds and gradually incorporate more sounds.

Usually I make use of sounds within the therapy location. These can be traffic noises, birds, people talking, fridges or computers humming, televisions, radios, etc. In addition, I ensure that the sounds come from different locations: some from a short distance away, others from further away, some from the left and others from the right. When we have established together what the sounds are, we then practise paying attention for around ten minutes, divided into three parts.

1. First, we spend four minutes with a selective focus on different individual sounds. I ask the client to focus fully on one of the sounds, for example the traffic on the road, and to focus on that noise in isolation for ten seconds. All the other sounds are now unimportant. Then they change their focus to another sound for ten seconds, for example the dishwasher, and the other sounds are now unimportant. The client continues in this way, with a ten-second focus on each of the individual sounds, for the period of four minutes.

2. For the next four minutes, the client moves between the sounds at a greater speed: two to four seconds per sound.

3. Towards the end of the exercise, the client spends two minutes on what I call 'divided attention'. That is to say, they try to divide or share their attention and focus equally on all the sounds at the same time.

At this stage, some clients are ready to take on greater challenges. For them I recommend introducing new sounds and more difficult sound combinations from one training session to the next. They can, for example, place high and low-pitched sounds together. They can also record their trigger thoughts on a mobile phone and play them back on a loop at the same time as the other sounds so as to learn to detach from the trigger thoughts by focussing on other sounds. (I use apps to do this: Voice Loop for iPhone and LoopStation for Android.)

In clinic, people often find it difficult to focus on the noises because they are more sensitive to the trigger thoughts and so 'hear' these louder than the external noises. When this occurs, I use a little exercise to illustrate our control over our attention. It is called the **windowpane exercise**. I stand with my client in front of a window in the clinic and ask them to write their trigger thoughts on the windowpane with a whiteboard pen. The trigger thoughts could be, for example, 'What is wrong with me?' 'I am worried that my colleagues don't like me.' 'Why am I feeling so sad?'

I ask my clients to focus fully on their trigger thoughts and to notice how the blue sky or the house opposite can be seen behind the ink of the pen but how these things are not as sharp as the writing. Afterwards, we change focus, looking between the thoughts to what they can see behind the text. Perhaps they notice trees in front of the house, cars on the street, or detailing on the windows of the house opposite. The client now notices how the trigger thoughts become a little less distinct. They are still there, they do not disappear, but the client can focus on other things and see past them. They then understand that they can control their attention.

Common pitfalls my clients encounter with the training include:

1. **They try to push certain sounds into the background and over-focus on other sounds.** They want to hear all the sounds all the time – including sounds which are not on the list of sounds which the client and I have selected together for them to focus in on. Perhaps they will find that the sounds to which they pay the least attention drop away into the

background a little, but this isn't the aim of the exercise. The aim is solely to focus in and pay attention to one sound at a time.

2. **They try to control their thoughts or feelings while training.** If they start to control their thoughts or feelings along the way, they should give up this control and repeat the exercise.

3. **They get dragged down by negative thoughts and frustrations.** Many of my clients have told me they get a bit upset during training and irritated by some of the sounds. They might get frustrated that some of the sounds are very faint or that too many of the sounds are similar. This is how it should be. The exercise is in learning to pay attention to – and then to detach attention from – external and internal sounds and thoughts, especially the negative, frustrating ones.

4. **They implement the techniques passively while they follow their daily routines, such as doing the washing, shopping and other things.** Instead they should give themselves time to focus on the training and do their daily tasks afterwards.

5. **They fall asleep or use the training to calm themselves down.** The aim is to consciously direct and redirect attention, not to relax.

C. BE MINDFUL BUT DETACHED

The opposite of ruminating is a state that Wells and Matthews called 'detached mindfulness'. This is a state where we observe our thought stream passively, like in the minutes before we fall asleep. We don't do anything with the thoughts – we just observe them. The opposite of rumination is thus not having an empty mind nor having fewer thoughts or only calm thoughts. We have up to 70,000 thoughts in a day. We cannot limit them, but we can avoid doing anything with them. Many of us find it very difficult to have thoughts and to do nothing with them. One of the exercises which can help us to achieve this state is what is known as the **tiger exercise**.

Start by thinking about a tiger. Really imagine what it looks like in detail so that you can *see* the tiger in front of you. With the tiger in the front of your mind, it takes up the space of other thoughts. Next, release control of the image; observe the tiger thought passively and see what happens. Perhaps the tiger will stay standing there; perhaps it will move around; perhaps it will disappear altogether. Regardless of what it does, you can release your control over the thought and leave it be.

If you do not try to make it disappear nor to stay, you will find that the tiger moves of its own accord.

The exercise shows that thoughts have their own lives if we observe them passively. This applies both to our imaginary tiger and to a thought like: 'Am I good enough?'

This may sound difficult, but I assure you that everyone is capable of detached mindfulness. For most of us this means that we are detached from our thoughts for most of the time. Think back to the thoughts that you had a few days ago on, say, Tuesday. Can you remember them? What became of the thought about what you should have for your evening meal?

If you dive into your stream of thought, you will discover that the majority of the thousands of thoughts you think each day just continue to move along the sushi belt. Who decides whether a thought is important or unimportant? Does the thought itself do this? No, of course not. Thoughts have no consciousness. They don't know whether they are important trigger thoughts or not. The thought 'maybe the TV programme is upsetting' doesn't know that it is less important than 'I am worried about ending up alone and lonely'. We make that evaluation. We are the masters of our own minds and responsible for the thoughts that we dwell on.

Let us look again at the sushi belt in front of us. A salmon maki, an avocado roll and a fried prawn move towards us ... do we have control over which items we reach out for and which we just observe and let pass us by? Yes, we do. It is the same with our stream of thought. Thoughts come and go. Sometimes the same thought will come by many times. We can choose just to observe it and let it pass us by on the belt.

The more we practise, the more experience we will have of detaching from our thoughts. And the more we experience detachment, the more we will believe that we have control over our ruminations.

▶ This is what I do in my clinic:

HOW TO BECOME GOOD AT JUST OBSERVING

In clinic I invite my clients to do an exercise in observing thoughts. I ask clients to settle themselves down and just allow all the thoughts that come into their heads to be there — without dwelling on them. I tell them just to observe the thoughts. They will perhaps discover that thoughts are fleeting, that there are pauses and gaps in the thought stream, or that thoughts have their own life. It is very common to have thoughts such as 'Why am I not having any thoughts?' and 'What a boring exercise'. It is also common to have thoughts which have nothing to do with the exercise, such as 'What shall I do this evening?' 'Why didn't my boss say anything about my work yesterday?' 'How can I tidy up my flat?'

Thought streams flow away, and one subject replaces another, if you don't choose to fixate and let yourself be carried away in the stream.

Attention can become erratic when you practise this exercise — one minute you are focussed on the coffee on the table, and the next minute you are listening to the cars driving by in the street. This is completely normal.

I introduce clients to the idea of varying the exercise by swapping between ruminating about the problems troubling them, and just observing the thoughts about their problems. This can happen in the following way:

1. First the client fills their head with trigger thoughts and for two minutes dives down into the thoughts about which they feel most strongly.

2. Then I ask them to release the trigger thoughts and use the next two minutes just to observe their thoughts. They should avoid following any of them but should just let them be.

When I do this exercise with a client, I ask them to change several times between ruminating and being mindfully detached; it is, I point out, like getting on and off a train again and again. After the exercise I ask the client what they have noticed and whether they can feel the difference between when they are ruminating and when they are detached.

Many of my clients describe a big difference – that during the two minutes when they ruminate about trigger thoughts, they think more and more, become sad and stressed, and get a knot in their stomach. The sadness and stress reduce correspondingly over the two minutes of detached mindfulness.

EVERYONE CAN LEARN TO DETACH THEIR ATTENTION

I am often asked: 'How do I know whether I will be able to learn to release my thoughts? What will happen if I do it wrong?'

If you have a tendency to ruminate a lot, it is not improbable that you will also begin to ruminate about the messages in this book and to speculate as to whether you too will be able to ruminate less: 'What will happen if I can't manage to let my thoughts be?'

In the metacognitive groups that we arrange in clinic, there are always people who start the process by ruminating on whether they are among the few who will not benefit from the therapy, who will not recover from sadness or depression in the course of working with the group: 'What will happen if I don't learn this method within six sessions of group therapy? What if I am a hopeless case? What if the others learn more quickly than me?' If they begin to ruminate a lot about whether or not they can manage to ruminate less, there is only one way out. This is to say to themselves: 'Now I will let this thought be, and if it is still running around my head at 8pm tonight I can ruminate about it then. Until then I will let the thought pass.'

▶ This is what I do in my clinic:

HOW TO REDUCE RUMINATION TIMES GRADUALLY – AND INCREASE DETACHED MINDFULNESS

Now and again people who I would call mega-ruminators come to me in clinic. They are used to spending most of their waking hours speculating about everything that is bothering them. It is especially difficult for them to reduce ruminating. It can seem completely impossible to go from ruminating for fifteen hours a day to one. I recommend to mega-ruminators that they gradually reduce their rumination time while increasing the time they spend practising detached mindfulness.

First, we agree that mega-ruminators should set themselves a target of ruminating for only one to two hours a day. We agree that they should not get angry with themselves if they feel it is hard, or if they sometimes revert back to ruminating for many hours. They just have to start again – with patience, as it takes time to change old habits. I often direct clients to remember when they learned to ride a bike and how they probably wobbled a lot and fell off several times before learning how to do it properly.

Then I introduce a six-day model to the client so they can slowly reduce rumination and increase detached mindfulness. The six-day model might look like this:

Day 1:
The client decides to practise detached mindfulness in the time between 8–9pm. During this time, they should let thoughts come and go without boarding the thought train and ruminating about them.

Day 2:
Today they should try to practise detached mindfulness from 7–9pm.

Day 3:
Now the client has to spend three hours a day practising detached mindfulness, from 6–9pm.

Day 4:
They are to use the time from 5–9pm for detached mindfulness.

Day 5:

Today they will undertake detached mindfulness from 4–9pm. This is when it starts to get really difficult, and clients often need to spend several days at the same stage before increasing the number of hours of detached mindfulness.

Day 6:

Now they expand their detached mindfulness to six consecutive hours over the course of the day.

After the client and I have followed the first six days in this process, the client continues by themselves until they have gone down to a maximum of two hours a day of rumination.

Everyone can learn to control whether they board their thought trains. For some people this can happen from one day to the next, for others it will take a little longer to learn.

When we get better at discovering trigger thoughts, become more aware of our ruminations and spend less time ruminating and more time being detached and attentive to life outside ourselves, we will find that we have more and more control over our ruminations. We will also find that we have greater *belief* in our self-control.

Our experiences throughout the process all go towards strengthening our belief in our own self-control, and the confidence this gives us creates a positive spiral.

There is, therefore, no reason to worry about how many trigger thoughts we still have. Life continuously, and completely automatically, contributes trigger thoughts which we can practise with. Every time we are faced with a challenge or disappointment, trigger thoughts we can practise with will follow.

Once we discover that we are in control of our ruminations, we can challenge ourselves to do things that we would normally have avoided for fear of uncomfortable trigger thoughts. This could, for example, involve having a difficult conversation with a partner or a friend, standing up to a colleague or a family member, or asking the boss for a pay rise. If we are afraid of having a difficult conversation with a friend, it may be because we still don't believe we can handle the difficult thoughts that might follow. But we can! And our experiences with limiting ruminations, whatever our thoughts and feelings, will mean that we will feel much stronger.

After my clients have experienced controlling their ruminations through metacognitive therapy, I bring back out the scale I used before and ask: 'How much do you now believe that you cannot control and limit your ruminations?'

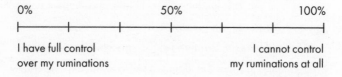

A response of 0 per cent means full control over ruminations. A response of 100 per cent means no control at all over ruminations.

Over the course of the therapy, nearly all my clients begin to believe that they can control their ruminations. When they have practised deferring rumination times, engaged in attention training and practised detached mindfulness over several weeks, their belief that they can control their ruminations prompts them to move to the left of the scale. They find that they have more control over the processes which keep despondency and depression alive.

METTE

'My head was full of ruminations
– night and day.'

On the first day back at work after the Christmas holidays in
January 2003 I was sitting in my car ready to drive to work.
While I was in the car, I suddenly felt really ill. I couldn't
breathe properly, everything was flickering in front of my
eyes, and all sounds seemed to be strangely far away. When I
arrived at work three hours later, I could hardly account for
how I got there.

I shut myself in my office and hoped that nobody would
want me for anything or ask me about anything. I just
couldn't think clearly.

When I got home from work that day, I broke down
completely. For the next two months I cried nearly all the
time, and I never went back to work. In the year before
the moment in the car (which turned out to be an anxiety
attack) I had developed problems sleeping.

I was working for an organisation which helped people
with special needs. The job was challenging. There were
many critical questions which had to be responded to every
day.

This made it difficult to set boundaries. You couldn't ask for a bit of peace and quiet to get your work finished and say: 'I'm sorry. I don't have time to talk to you. You will just have to wait a few days.' I worked 40–50 hours a week and, with two hours' drive on top of that each way, it made for very long days.

The comedown after the anxiety attack was terrible: I couldn't find the calm I needed to relax but was unable to find the concentration to do anything either. All I did was sit. I slept at most one hour a day during the first two months and felt I had gone 'crazy'. I had suicidal thoughts and felt constantly stressed and depressed.

I was very scared about not being able to control my body. That I would just be sat there and my body would not let me get up. Or that my body did not want to sleep even though I laid down. I really couldn't understand what was going on. At that time, stress was not as well-known as it is today, so I couldn't understand why my body reacted so violently. For example, I had a lot of pain in my arms. It felt as though my blood was too thick. I also had severe memory loss. I couldn't remember people's names. I couldn't remember certain words. Now I know that all these were symptoms of stress.

I talked things through with a psychologist

The doctor recommended I take medication, but I didn't want to do that, so instead I was given an appointment to talk to a psychologist.

We talked mostly about stress, why it occurs and how I could avoid getting stressed again. We talked about my work, how that had affected me, and how my daily life should now function for me. We also talked about my suicidal thoughts as I was very afraid they would recur.

I was really glad to see the psychologist, and I am sure that if I had not spoken with her I would have taken my own life. So, you could say that the discussion saved my life. But it didn't make me happy again. My quality of life was poor, and the difficulties I had experienced as a result of stress – including the poor memory – did not disappear. My memory improved very slowly and worsened again as soon as I got even a little bit stressed.

I also started attending a stress course on which we were taught that we should stop becoming stressed. But how do you do that? I did not feel as though I was stressed, since I was not working and was not the sort of person who slaved away in the house. I was only just about getting my housework done.

I was on sick leave for a year. I reported to the local authority and underwent a fitness for work test at one of the local authority offices, since I had left my previous job.

Things got tolerable again. But I was still very tearful (among other things, I would sit in the shower and bawl), and my sleep pattern was completely destroyed. I couldn't sleep in my own bed or next to anyone, so I spent more or less every night on the sofa.

In and out of depression

After this followed a few years with great fluctuations – in terms of my mental health and my day to day quality of life. There were periods when I was reasonably okay. I was headhunted for a flexible job and was glad and honoured to receive this offer. At other times the suicidal thoughts came back, and I was thankful for medication since I was even less keen on the alternative: admission to a psychiatric hospital.

It seemed like the medication produced a good effect immediately as my suicidal thoughts disappeared. So, I stopped seeing the psychologist and started work at the flexible job.

But during the first few days of work, things weren't as good as I had hoped they would be. I felt I was being singled out for bullying by two female colleagues who were leaving me out of things socially. When I came home from work in the afternoons, I would think about what the two of them had said during the day, and why they had done this and that. I was irritated at myself for being the weird stressed person who couldn't function normally. I was afraid that the bullying would never stop and that it was my own fault. And I felt that I should be able to pull myself together.

I tried to control my thoughts and convince myself that 'it was just a bit of nonsense'. I thought 'Are you sure it is not just you misunderstanding something?' and 'You should just be indifferent to it'.

But, despite this attempt to pull myself together, I began to feel worse and worse. Every afternoon after work

I crawled onto the sofa and speculated about whether I had done something wrong during the day, whether I had said the wrong thing, behaved in the wrong way. The social life which I had been building up again after the first depression once more fell apart, and I blamed myself for doing badly again.

Since I was no longer going to the psychologist, who could have said to me that things *were* going wrong and that it was not all just in my head, I could not see for myself what was wrong. I was so inward focussed. I spent a huge amount of time thinking about it. I tried several times to come off the medication, but every time I felt just terrible and had to start again. One day at work I locked myself in the toilet and broke down. And so, I ended up with depression again.

Thoughts and nightmares filled my whole life. I upped the medication and began to go and see the psychologist again, which resulted in a whole lot of new things emerging about work, which I had ignored. I gained an understanding of some of the bad experiences, but thinking about all those things didn't make me any better. Every time things got bad for me, I once again started to think about whether the bullying was all my fault. I often felt a bit better for the hour I was sat with the psychologist, and perhaps for a few days after, but then things would be really bad again.

My journey into the metacognitive world

At a certain point I came across a group on Facebook where other people were describing similar experiences of bullying, nightmares and flashbacks. Here I also read about metacognitive therapy, which I thought sounded interesting, and I began an intensive metacognitive therapy group course.

At the first group therapy session I was amazed that we didn't have to talk about our experiences at all. Instead we talked about our thoughts. This was a very different form of therapy for me. What came out of it is that I am not especially sensitive, as I had been told elsewhere. I am instead extremely inward-focussed – focussed on myself and on the threats I feared. I learned that I myself can choose to focus outwards and not inwards, and I learned to be what was referred to as *detached* – creating distance between myself and the thoughts.

When I went home after the first group therapy session, I was more in the present than I had been for a long time. I ruminated less and was suddenly not so tired anymore. I began to be able to sleep again. When you come home after a three-hour therapy session and notice such an effect you do think: 'No, this can't be happening.' But it can!

I found out that what worked well was not to jump on my trigger thoughts when they came. Instead I had to set aside a limited time for worrying. When a negative trigger thought came, I had to wait until this time. So, I agreed a time in the evening with myself when I could worry if I wanted, but when I got to the evening, strangely enough there were no thoughts to worry about. Before, I would have gone and ruminated for a week in advance of a meeting or engagement. I would have wanted to think and speculate – not anything constructive, just thinking. Now I have a plan of action for myself, which says when I can think about such things. The rest of the time my heart is free – not free from thoughts, as they still come when it suits them, but free from having to deal with them. This is a relief. I use the same technique when I am out among other people. I don't constantly wonder what they think about me. That must wait until the set time.

The greatest change for me has been the feeling of control. Being able to regain control over my body and thoughts.

The feeling of not being in control is very unpleasant. Especially as I was very depressed and suicidal. It was terrible. So, it is fantastic to notice that I just have to focus on something else and I feel better. I am no longer dependent on doctors and psychologists. That is incredibly positive. I want to take responsibility for my life – I just didn't know how to. I use strategies with an outward focus every single day and it feels as though I have got my life back.

I have now come off all medication, and I know that this time is different. I now know the cause of depression and can control the mechanisms myself.

METTE'S JOURNEY FROM TRIGGER THOUGHTS TO DEPRESSION

Mette, who suffered from depression, stress and social anxiety, was a victim of workplace bullying. Her trigger thoughts were negative thoughts about herself and concern that other people didn't like her. Trigger thoughts occurred especially when she was with other people. Mette worried all day, including at night, and this led to poor sleep, nightmares and low self-esteem.

TRIGGER THOUGHTS	CAS RESPONSES	MOOD/SYMPTOMS
• What do others think? • Why can't I just pull myself together? • Why am I such a stressed person?	• Turning thoughts over and over • Thinking positive • Avoiding social situations • Passivity **TIME SPENT:** • The whole day	• Depressive • Low self-esteem • Tearful • Concentration problems • Tiredness • Sleep problems • Nightmares

METTE'S OLD STRATEGIES WHICH CONTRIBUTED TO HER SYMPTOMS	METTE'S NEW STRATEGIES WHICH OVERCAME HER SYMPTOMS
Thinking style: I was really thinking a lot about interactions with other people and was constantly worried about the past, present and future.	**Thinking style:** I have introduced a fixed rumination time every day at 5pm. More often than not, however, I don't need my rumination time.
Focus of attention: My focus was on all the negatives that I could find to think about. How people behaved towards me. Whether I was good enough in comparison with them. Fear of loneliness. I constantly analysed past events.	**Focus of attention:** My attention is focussed on the present and on doing things that I enjoy. I am paying attention to enjoying life.
Behaviour: I took part in a very limited number of social events so as to avoid further worries about and conflicts with other people. I isolated myself and was constantly tired.	**Behaviour:** I have much more energy and a much clearer view of things. I sleep better, resolve conflicts better and have higher self-esteem. I am back out living my life again.

What I have learned about my thoughts:

I have learned that I can decide for myself what I will think about and for how long. I have learned that overthinking was making me ill.

CHAPTER 4

RUMINATION IS (JUST) A HABIT

Growing up, we learn to use our intellect to analyse problems. We learn to think things over before making a decision. As such, we come to regard ruminations as useful. Being able to think analytically is indeed a useful skill to have. In our relationships with other people, as well as when we face a challenging situation on our own, we need to be able to see things from several viewpoints and weigh them up against one another. But the habit of analysing every problem in great detail can stand in the way of us ever taking action – particularly when it comes to life's emotional challenges. Analysis can end up taking over to such an extent that it worsens our mood and causes symptoms of depression.

In this chapter, I want to challenge anyone who analyses things a lot and who has become dejected about this to ask themselves: 'What use are my ruminations?' In my clinic, using the following scale, I ask my clients to evaluate the extent to which their ruminations answer their questions or provide solutions to their problems and symptoms of depression.

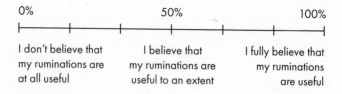

0%	50%	100%
I don't believe that my ruminations are at all useful	I believe that my ruminations are useful to an extent	I fully believe that my ruminations are useful

My clinical experience shows that ruminations serve no useful purpose and can often maintain depressive symptoms. If you occupy yourself too much with thoughts, you can become tangled up in them and unable to move on to anything else. Adrian Wells illustrates this with a question: 'Is it possible to hold a door closed and walk away from it at the same time?' The benefits of limiting rumination, on the other hand, can be notable: more joy in life, greater self-esteem and a more functional and creative brain.

Some of my clients do not regard rumination as problematic, which can allow depressive symptoms to develop. They regard it as just a means of problem-solving and reflection. It can therefore feel counterintuitive to them to cut back on rumination time to improve their mood. I challenge these clients to test themselves with a little experiment. For four weeks they are to reduce their rumination time as though they were taking a kind of long holiday. Afterwards they can return to ruminating for longer periods of the day if they prefer. The majority experience a positive effect from thinking less. They get a taste for a rumination-free life and end up not wanting to come home from their holiday.

The idea that rumination is the route to solutions is deeply entrenched in many of us. In the following section we'll explore some of the most frequent arguments my clients make in the clinic in support of rumination.

'Focusing on problems leads me to a solution to my depression.'

I often meet clients who, in an attempt to escape from their symptoms of depression, have considered and tried out all manner of different therapies and self-help. But far from resulting in an improvement, this excessive focus on problem-solving actually keeps the symptoms alive because the time-consuming attempt to relieve the depression often involves more thinking. Many people use alternative treatments to try to cure their depression, such as prayer, retreats, writing therapy, yoga, Qigong or mindfulness-meditation. But, while these activities can increase well-being, health and happiness, there is no particularly good evidence that they can help us to recover from despondency and depression in the long term. Likewise, 'all-in-one therapies', where several methods are combined, have not been found to be as effective as pure metacognitive therapy.

'Self-criticism minimises my mistakes.'

Some of my clients think it is useful to criticise themselves: 'Why can't I do anything without getting it wrong?' They feel that mentally beating themselves up will make them more alert to their failings, such that they will make fewer mistakes in the future. But this is not the way to address the problem. However angry we get with ourselves for making a mistake, we will still make new mistakes in the future. We cannot live our lives without making mistakes, and we don't make fewer mistakes by ruminating about them.

'Rumination protects me against the bad times.'

For some people, rumination is a form of protection against disappointment, failure and despondency. They ruminate themselves into the depths of depression, as they are convinced that they are not worth anything and therefore they cannot fall any deeper. At the bottom of this black hole they feel they are of such little value that even if people were to criticise them and point out their failings, they would not feel hurt because they have already hit rock bottom. This strategy is damaging. Rumination can protect us from being disappointed, but it robs us of our reserves of energy, good mood, self-esteem and general quality of life.

'My rumination leads to better decisions.'

When people have to make an important decision, they may feel that they should ruminate about the pros and cons, and some mega-ruminators consider the pros and cons for years before coming to a decision. The fact is that our decisions are seldom better after ruminating for months on end; instead we often end up more depressed and confused in the long run.

'Rumination is a source of creativity and new ideas.'

I recently had an artist come to me for therapy. He was very thoughtful and convinced that he needed to ruminate a lot to access his creativity. He therefore spent most of the day speculating about love, politics and the structure and challenges of society. He delighted in this overthinking and even thought of it as a part of his personality and identity.

There was just one problem. In addition to bringing him joy and energy, this process also brought him stress and depression.

My client faced a dilemma: should he continue with his daily ruminations, which typically lasted between eight and twelve hours, in order to preserve his creativity (as he saw it), or should he reduce his thinking time and therefore reduce his symptoms of depression? The artist was convinced that he was required to 'pay the price with depression' in order to preserve his creativity. Was he right?

We discussed how he might still stimulate his creativity while reducing rumination and decided that, instead of spending twelve hours a day creative ruminating, he would spend two hours a day, between 10 and 12am: a morning shot of creative adrenalin. If a thought or emotion that could spark a creative idea should occur to him at 4pm, he should have the confidence that – if the thought were important enough – it would strike him again the next morning.

Initially he was sceptical about the plan and did not think he would be able to learn to reduce his thinking, which, he believed, was such an integral part of his personality.

But in metacognitive therapy he learned to activate the passive observation of his thought flow, to practise detached mindfulness. He discovered that if an idea was good, it did return the next morning without him having to write it down or try to hold on to it. He also discovered that he had just as many thoughts and ideas, retained his artistic creativity and was able to create fantastic pieces of work without being depressed.

Many of us want to ruminate and philosophise from time to time. I myself am one of them. We like to philosophise about everything, think out new projects and brainstorm creative ideas. For me – like for lots of other people – this analysis brings great pleasure. I love to fantasise about which research projects I should tackle, which books or columns I should write, or what I should say at an important interview. But I am aware that these ruminations must not completely take over, and I am also very aware of the need to practise detached mindfulness every day. Even more important: I believe 100 per cent in my control over ruminations, regardless of internal and external events. This feeling of control makes me stronger and means that I may well only ruminate deeply once in a while.

'Positive rumination increases my self-esteem.'

Some people think that rumination can be the route to increased self-esteem. If we just accept ourselves more or repeat positive or self-loving words to ourselves, we believe that self-esteem is reinforced. However, high self-esteem is not built up by thinking; on the contrary, we undermine it by thinking. We have a high level of self-esteem in childhood, and if we continue to limit our ruminations we can preserve this throughout our lives.

We all feel from time to time that we are less clever, less beautiful or less successful than other people. At these times we pay extra attention to those who have achieved success and a high level of self-confidence. And we think that only when we ourselves become as successful can we escape our low self-esteem and depressive symptoms.

But high self-esteem does not directly follow on from success nor from repeating positive mantras or thinking positive thoughts about ourselves. Everyone has negative thoughts about themselves sometimes. We all make mistakes at work and criticise ourselves for them. We all experience disappointment which can make us sad, and we ask ourselves if we could have done things differently. Despite this, we don't all have low self-esteem. It is thus not the negative thoughts or beliefs themselves which rob us of our self-esteem but our strategies for dealing with those negative beliefs. It is possible to know that something is negative without turning it over in our minds for hours on end.

Seldom can we think our way to higher self-esteem in the long term – not by writing a positivity diary, turning negative thoughts into positive ones, or repeating positive mantras and inner pep talks to ourselves such as: 'You are good enough. You have nice hair. All your friends love you.' These strategies might have an immediate effect, but it is short-lived and requires constant maintenance to continue being effective.

'Ruminating is my core identity. Who am I without it?'

It can be difficult to reconcile ourselves to the thought process in metacognitive therapy if we experience intense rumination every day and depression as part of our personality, like the artist did. I sometimes meet people who feel themselves to be particularly analytical, melancholic, deep-feeling or sensitive, and who feel that these characteristics define their personality.

They are afraid to stop ruminating since they feel they will end up losing themselves. Even if the ruminations lead to symptoms of depression, they feel they are in a secure and familiar place; they're like the old smelly slippers which we know we should throw out but which we keep nevertheless in the hall. We need to recognise that our rumination is not our core identity but an inconvenient habit which we can change. We will still be ourselves – just a new version of ourselves with less ruminating and depression.

In therapy I ask my clients to complete this form on the perceived advantages and disadvantages of deep rumination. Included in this example are typical responses my clients provide.

ADVANTAGES OF RUMINATING	DISADVANTAGES OF RUMINATING
• Ruminating may lead me to solutions or answers. • Ruminating gives me insight into myself. • Ruminating enables me to make more considered decisions. • Ruminating makes me deep and creative.	• Ruminating ruins my sleep. • Ruminating destroys my self-esteem. • Ruminating keeps my despondency and depression alive. • Ruminating is tiring and takes away my ability to be present. • Ruminating takes me away from my family and friends.

After I have run through all of the arguments for and against rumination with clients, and once they have filled in the form, more often than not it becomes clear that the disadvantages of ruminating far outweigh the advantages. Depression is a high price to pay for greater self-insight or a creative personality. After analysis I usually ask the client to reconsider the extent to which they now believe their rumination is useful. Often their answer moves further to the left on the scale below. That is to say, their belief in the use and value of rumination diminishes.

With this insight it is easier to limit ruminations – including in the long term.

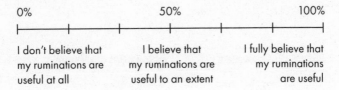

0%	50%	100%
I don't believe that my ruminations are useful at all	I believe that my ruminations are useful to an extent	I fully believe that my ruminations are useful

LEIF

'I was convinced that I had to process the dark thoughts in order to move forward.'

I have suffered with depression since my teenage years. My thoughts, which often centred around death, never completely floored me – neither as a young person nor in the first few years of adulthood. I got an education and a job, got married and had children – and I accepted that the dark thoughts were my lot in life.

There were periods when I was in a vicious circle. I couldn't escape from the thought that I was going to die. But I did nothing about it. I believe that at some level I accepted that I should go through life being afraid of this.

I got on with my work and family life and never received any treatment.

Then, when I was in my late thirties, I got a new job at a company with a highly competitive working culture. There was something in this culture which attracted me. I took the bait and began to work really hard, and I even achieved some results which caught the attention of the management.

But my problems came when I took time off work. I could not enjoy holidays. I was straight away hit by worries and anxieties, and I felt really terrible. All I wanted to do was to go back to work. Work was my medicine. It kept my energy levels up.

Depressive tendencies in everyday life

After some years, the anxiety-filled and depressive thoughts which I experienced while on holidays moved into my everyday life, and I ended up having to take sick leave. My doctor diagnosed me with depression; I got some medication and began to talk to a psychologist.

The discussions with the psychologist were just like having a general chat with someone, which I don't feel I got a lot out of. But I did get better and believed that the medication was helping, until I had a relapse on a holiday.

In the years which followed, my working life was unstable. I moved to another town where I got a new job with reduced hours. I also started to study but then stopped that and got another job instead. After some time, I took up my course again, and I got some flexible jobs, but I struggled the whole time with dark thoughts and anxiety around death. These thoughts filled my head to an extreme degree. I was afraid to die, and it was like a self-fulfilling prophecy. Because I was going to *have* to die, I also *had* to think about it. That is what it was like for me. But I wasn't living my life. The thoughts took over everything. It was like a living death. I felt as though I was in hell. When you are in a state of depression, it takes over and becomes problematic in itself.

I tried several types of therapy, but the thoughts kept on coming, and I was convinced that I should spend time on them when they came. Otherwise why would they come?

The basic premises of metacognitive therapy were completely new.

When I was introduced to metacognitive therapy, I also had my reservations.

The basic premise stated that everyone has negative and dark thoughts but not everyone cultivates them.

It was explained to me that I didn't need to feel so bad all the time. I had always believed that this was just how it was for me. I had always felt that I had to analyse these thoughts. And that I had absolutely no choice about it.

Now I learned that I didn't have to go into these dark thoughts, that I should just release them and wait to see if they returned. I learned that I could sit in an armchair at home and tell myself that I didn't want to cultivate them.

The turning point came when, after a few sessions, I discovered that I was actually succeeding in letting the thoughts come and go, without it spoiling my day – and without things developing into a dark downturn.

I still believe that I will encounter sadness. But I am better at moving forward, which means I am not afraid of having another episode of severe depression. My life is not ruined by a couple of dark thoughts. I have managed to release the dark thoughts and move on. They do still come. And sometimes they come often, but I get on with my life and my stuff. I don't need to sit and wallow in them. I used to believe this was something I had to do. The idea that I didn't have to do this was very new to me.

I have now completely escaped from depression. I have a stable job, greater emotional reserves and greater self-esteem.

LEIF'S JOURNEY FROM TRIGGER THOUGHTS TO DEPRESSION

Since he was young, Leif suffered from depression and anxiety about death. His trigger thoughts – including hopelessness and a bad conscience about his family – typically arose in the mornings and set in motion six to eight hours of rumination in the search for a solution. The long hours spent ruminating caused tiredness, concentration problems and poor sleep.

TRIGGER THOUGHTS	CAS RESPONSES	MOOD/SYMPTOMS
• How do I deal with death? • Will things ever get better for me? • Where is the joy in living?	• Finding answers • Speculating • Praying to God • Analysing • Mood monitoring • Staying in bed **TIME SPENT:** • 6–8 hours a day	• Depression • Hopelessness • Anxiety • Concentration problems • Tiredness • Sleep problems

LEIF'S OLD STRATEGIES WHICH TRIGGERED SYMPTOMS	LEIF'S NEW STRATEGIES WHICH OVERCAME SYMPTOMS
Thinking style:	**Thinking style:**
I felt obliged to think death through.	I know now that I don't have to think about death and other negative things. I don't need to delve into negative thoughts.
Focus for attention:	**Focus for attention:**
My attention was focussed on myself and on my inner thoughts. I was often absent when in the company of others. When I was with other people, I often sat apart from them and ruminated.	My attention is on the outside world. I have an external focus now, for example, on my family and my work.
Behaviour:	**Behaviour:**
I talked to other people about my thoughts and tried alternative solutions, such as healing.	I keep to a schedule for the day regardless of mood, thoughts and feelings. I get on with things even if I feel reluctant and lack motivation.

What I have learned about my thoughts:

I no longer believe that my dark thoughts have to be processed. I don't have to ruminate about negative thoughts.

CHAPTER 5

GET OUT OF YOUR HEAD AND INTO YOUR LIFE

Most people dream of change. We dream about learning to play the piano. Or about moving to the country and becoming self-sufficient. Or building a community, taking a new course or finding a job in a completely different sector. We fantasise about one day being able to cook all the recipes from the cookbooks we have bought over the years but have never really got into using. We dream about picking up new hobbies, taking up old ones again or getting to know new people with common interests. People who suffer from sadness, despondency or depression have just as many dreams as everyone else; however, I often see in clients that the fear of a new depression or period of dark thoughts stands in the way of making their dreams a reality. They want to make plans for the future, but they dread making a mistake or having a bad experience and are convinced that a new bout of depression will destroy their motivation, and so they rarely follow through on plans.

In those who suffer from depression or from recurring episodes, it is very common that the fear of becoming depressed or down again can develop into an *expectation* that this will happen. Their ruminations centre on this expectation: 'I can't avoid getting depressed again. I feel that I am slightly more upset about this today than I was yesterday. I can remember this feeling of anxiety from the last time I got depressed.' Ruminations of this type can convince us that depressive symptoms are a condition of our lives. It is as though it is our lot in life to be depressed or at constant risk of becoming depressed. We come to believe that we have a more unstable psyche than other people. So, we choose to hold ourselves back. We avoid seeking out new experiences for fear of not being able to manage them. And instead we choose the safe option and live life in the slow lane.

My mission is to show people through metacognitive therapy that even people who have been depressed can live a very full life. It is possible to escape from these restricting fears and expectations. Just like breaking any bad habit, it requires patience and focus. If over many years we have got used to saying no to plans and have only spent time in environments where we feel safe, our internal control system needs to be restructured and reset so that we are able to reach out and grasp life's possibilities in the same way as other people – even those possibilities which right now seem unattainable.

There are several steps on this journey to get out of our head and into our life. First and foremost, we need to be aware of our rumination and believe that we can control it, regardless of what life presents by way of challenges, defeats and negative thoughts – as we've explored in the preceding chapters.

The next step in metacognitive therapy is to recognise that we *can* live out our dreams and that we *can* stick to an action plan, regardless of our thoughts and feelings. Many people find that ruminating less frees up a lot of time, making it possible to turn their dreams into reality. I usually ask my clients how they would most like to use the extra time. If depression has been a part of life for years, then it can be hard to know what we really want. Do you harbour an old dream to run your own business? Or do you just want to begin every morning with a smile instead of a struggle to face the day? Once we discover our dream, we have to make a plan. Perhaps it is just a plan for the next few hours; perhaps it is a plan that involves sweeping changes to our life. Both plans can be carried out – even if motivation disappears along the way. Depression and dejection are not a person's lot in life.

Dreams and wishes come about when we take part in life. Imagine that you are standing in front of a large, well-prepared buffet in a five-star hotel. There are mussels in white wine, glazed and dry-cured hams, and seasonal vegetable risotto. There are fresh salads and sweet tomatoes, Chanterelle mushrooms and new potatoes. There are delicious cheeses, cakes, fruit and nuts. You might be able to imagine how things will taste. But you won't know what they really taste like until you try them. You must first take a step forward and pick up a plate.

It is the same with life and all the possibilities it offers. Do you want to go to university, change jobs, find a partner or switch to working part-time so as to free up time for creative activities? Well, jump to it! This can feel like a provocative challenge. How can you jump into life when you have spent years protecting yourself with completely the opposite strategy?

If you have spent many hours a day ruminating – and have been a mega-ruminator – it can be very difficult to convince yourself that the future does not have to be limited by the threat of new depression. But when you discover that you can limit the ruminations that keep depression alive and when you accept that you are not a victim of genetics, the time of year or oversensitivity, you will free up a lot of time.

HOW TO ACT WITHOUT MOTIVATION

One of the key elements of metacognitive therapy is learning how to act without motivation. It is vital to be able to learn to do things, and stick to a plan, even when you are not motivated.

Our motivation and desire are dynamic and can change from day to day – and sometimes from hour to hour. If it is gloomy outside, or if we are having a bad week, it is normal for our motivation to get out of bed, exercise or see other people to decrease drastically. Suddenly we don't look forward to our walk in the woods, watching our favourite TV show or making something nice for dinner. We might give ourselves a pep talk to re-ignite this desire, or we might decide to stay in bed and wait for our motivation to return. Both strategies risk further rumination.

We do hundreds of things every day without feeling any desire or motivation. Personally, I am not motivated to wash up after the evening meal, nor to tidy up the house or clean my teeth before bedtime.

But I do it anyway. I don't wait for the motivation to appear. When I think back to this morning, I was not particularly motivated to get out of bed. I wanted to sleep for a little longer. Many people want to carry on lying in bed when the alarm goes off. But we know that the best strategy is to get up and go to our job or appointment.

Thoughts, feelings and actions are three different things that don't necessarily coexist. We undertake hundreds of tasks every day without feeling any motivation, and we make hundreds of movements without thinking about them. The vast majority of our actions have nothing to do with thoughts and feelings, but we do them anyway. For instance, if I were to wait to be motivated to go to the gym, I would never go. Likewise, I don't wait to go to the supermarket until I feel excited to go. The best strategy is to practise following an action plan without relating it so much to motivation, feelings and thoughts.

Let's think about the example of getting out of bed in the morning. The alarm goes off at 7am. Our motivation to remove ourselves from the snug duvet and move into the bathroom is just about nil. What do we do?

There are several possible reactions. Our strategy determines whether it is easy for us to get out of bed, or not:

Strategy no. 1:

We continue to lie there and wait for the desire to get up to show itself. This is not a good strategy. It provides the ideal conditions for ruminating, plunging us deeper into the tiredness and dejection that we woke up with.

Strategy no. 2:

We try to suppress thoughts, to bury them or to chase them out of our head. This strategy will backfire. It consumes energy, and the thoughts will keep popping up again and again just like the rubber duck that we try to push down under the bathwater.

Strategy no. 3:

We try to pep talk ourselves out of bed – to give ourselves enticements like hot coffee or the rays of morning sunshine. This strategy is not terribly good either. The internal debate creates more worry in our head, and we risk convincing ourselves that it is best to stay in bed, despite the aim having been to convince ourselves otherwise. 'Come on now, it's going to be a good day,' says one thought. 'Oh no it won't. I don't have the strength for today,' says the other. We cannot be sure that the pep talk thoughts will win this debate. The pep talk is 'active thinking', and, as we've seen, overthinking cannot be solved with more thinking, even if the thoughts are positive.

Strategy no. 4:

Another common strategy is that we attempt to pull ourselves together by rebuking ourselves for being such a lazy person who can't get up in the mornings. It is possible for self-criticism to get us going, but self-esteem and a good mood will disappear along the way. It is not possible to ruminate ourselves into better habits. Therefore, this strategy is not particularly good.

Strategy no. 5:

The best strategy is to be detached from thoughts. We focus on the plan to get up and ignore our lack of desire and motivation. When we focus on the plan, the background music of unmotivated thoughts will quietly fade away.

The more we stick to the plan and do things without giving ourselves a pep talk to get into a motivated mindset, or giving ourselves a choice to deviate from the plan, the more we will find we can act regardless of our thoughts and feelings. We can go into town even though we would prefer to stay at home, and we can go to the gym even though we would prefer to stay on the sofa watching TV. We learn to separate thoughts and actions.

IT IS NOT EITHER/OR, BUT BOTH/AND

The human mind functions in a much more sophisticated manner than most of us realise. Many of us tend to regard our condition as an either/or system: either we are 100 per cent depressed and only have the energy to sit and wait for an improvement, or else we are completely on top of things. But this is not how the mind works. We can easily experience several opposing feelings at the same time: we can feel happy and sad; we can feel love and hate. Nothing is just either/or but typically both/and.

That is to say, we can easily have trigger thoughts in our heads and not feel great physically but at the same time enjoy a good film at the cinema. The one does not preclude the other. Desire and action are not mutually exclusive either. We can easily take action without desire. Many of my clients tell me that they stop noticing their trigger thoughts when, despite a lack of desire or motivation, they push themselves to go to work or to social occasions. Even if they want to say no to an invitation, they go anyway and end up having a lovely and fun evening. They tell me that a party – despite their initial lack of desire to go along – often succeeds in drawing them away from their focus on their own thoughts and instead puts them in a better mood. Some people tell me too that they experience the background music of negative thoughts about problems and fear at the same time as having a good time at a party. Thus, it is not either/or but both/and.

▶ **This is what I do in my clinic:**

HOW TO PRACTISE ACTING WITHOUT MOTIVATION

It is very common for people to find it difficult to do things they don't want to do, but the ability to act without motivation comes with practice. Together the client and I make a list of the things the client has to do without wanting to. This could include:

- Eating

- Getting out of bed

- Talking to someone

- Lying down to rest

- Going for a walk

- Emptying the dishwasher.

When clients discover that they can easily do all these things without focussing their thoughts and feelings on wanting to do them, it means they can start to introduce activities on fixed days and take important decisions on time, regardless of their mood or mindset.

Some clients tell me that they resolve to get up at 7am every day, eat their meals at 8am, noon and 6pm, and go for a walk for a minimum of ten minutes every afternoon. Other clients decide that they will meet up with at least two people every week. They will have coffee with a neighbour, eat breakfast with a friend, or go for a walk with a colleague. Over time they find that they can maintain a stable level of activity, regardless of whether they are having a good or bad day.

I challenge my clients to increase the level of difficulty of 'acting without motivation' exercises by asking themselves every third day:

'What do I least want to do right now?' and then going and doing precisely that. In this way they discover that they can follow an action plan without any motivation. With experience, they build up the strength that will enable them, for example, to follow a course of education, or to stay in a job or a relationship, where their feelings of desire and motivation are sure to fluctuate over time.

SEPARATE THOUGHTS AND ACTIONS TO CREATE MOMENTUM

Even the most crucial decisions in life can be made without the right mindset or 100 per cent clarity.

Making major decisions is rarely straightforward. As a starting point, it is good to look at the matter in question from different angles before making a decision. If you are considering resigning from your job because you are not thriving in the workplace, then you will presumably consider the economy, options for finding a new job, the good colleagues you will miss and the security of your usual daily routine. All these thoughts can hold you back from your first impulse: to resign. Another example that clients often mention is the wish to leave their spouse because the marriage is not as strong as it once was. For example, the client recounts that, despite the bad marriage, she holds back from making a break for fear of regretting it and for fear of how it may affect the children. But neither does she choose to remain and fight for the marriage; instead goes into a state of limbo and ruminates about the possibilities. She is in the marriage but without conviction. While most people will eventually decide either to stay and pull out all the stops to get the best out of the marriage or to get divorced, mega-ruminators remain in limbo.

People who ruminate a lot find it much more difficult to come to a decision than others. Mega-ruminators addition-ally tend to ruminate about the ruminations: 'Why can't I just make a decision? Why do I keep changing my mind?' The new ruminations can confuse the original problem. Some people use inappropriate rules with regard to these dilemma-focussed ruminations, and so it becomes hard to take action. If we can-not deal with a dilemma until we feel 100 per cent convinced about our choice, we risk becoming trapped in ruminations without any momentum behind them. The best strategy is not to wait to act until we have settled on a decision – as when will we be settled? In two weeks? Two years? Or never. A much more robust rule is to limit rumination time and to act within a set timeframe.

In my clinic I use the three-step model detailed below as a starting point when teaching my clients how to take action on the basis of a fixed timeframe. We adjust the plans in line with the individual's own schedule, but I always discourage extending the timeframe.

1. The client sets herself a timeframe – for example, three months – in which to complete the exercise. She determines that she will spend an hour a day for three months analysing the situation. In the allotted hour she concentrates on thinking through all aspects of the situation.

2. After three months, she makes a decision. Now she has to act, even if she doesn't feel that the answer is clear-cut. If she is considering divorce, then she must either get a divorce or commit to staying in the marriage.

3. If, after she has taken the decision, she has trigger thoughts doubting whether she has made the right decision, she should decide to apply detached mindfulness to these thoughts. She must not let herself get carried away and ruminate about them, but just let the thoughts come and go. I recommend allocating an hour a day at most to analyse her thoughts about doubts, and to observe the thoughts passively if they crop up outside the allocated period of time. Now we establish a timeframe – for example a month or six months – in which to evaluate her decision. If, after this period of detached mindfulness, she is still in doubt, then she must start over and go through the three-step model again.

This is not an easy exercise. Some people never find a clear answer to life's big decisions. You can in the meantime succeed in living a good life without depressive symptoms, even if you cannot quite make up your mind about what you definitely want or cannot make important decisions.

Through metacognitive therapy you will discover that it is easy to take doubts to work, to the cinema or to visit a friend. You can in fact be happy and cheerful while at the same time having doubts lurking in the background. The most important thing is not to get rid of doubts but to discover that you can control your ruminations and live a meaningful and depression-free life despite them.

BERIT

'Metacognitive therapy was a lightbulb moment.'

I was at my second session of metacognitive therapy when
the psychologist asked: 'Do you think your depression has
caused your ruminations, or do you think your ruminations
have caused your depression?'

That clicked with me – it was completely clear.
Obviously, my thinking was the problem. I thought all the
time about whether I was doing things well enough and
whether other people liked me. I worried the whole time
about whether I was succeeding at work and at home.
Sometimes I didn't even want to speak to my children
because I was so taken up with thinking. They were really
burdensome thoughts which I couldn't bear. And when I sat
there with the psychologist, and I understood that it was all
my thinking which was feeding the depression, it was a real
lightbulb moment of realisation and a big surprise, because
for my whole life I had been convinced that it was better for
you to delve into things more deeply.

During my working life I have worked with families
and children who need help and support. It is a very
rewarding but mentally demanding job, and part of the
job is to supervise and be supervised. I have also visited

a psychologist several times to help me structure and talk about my feelings and thoughts. I have tried cognitive therapy, positive psychology, mindfulness and yoga. I was satisfied with these to start with. They worked within the systems I was used to, both at work and in my private life. I had never thought it could be any different. So, I was amazed that the psychologist using metacognitive therapy was not interested in hearing more about the content of my thoughts.

I went to see a metacognitive therapist because I suffered a second breakdown with stress. Both times I had a very heavy depressing feeling of powerlessness and fear about the future, which followed in the wake of the stress.

The first time I suffered from stress I had a shock. I had never experienced anything like it. We had all sorts of challenges at work with disputes, cutbacks and the like. I went downhill rapidly: I couldn't breathe, couldn't go to work, couldn't walk like I used to. My body gave up completely. In the same period, my sister-in-law died, and a whole lot of family challenges arose in connection with her death. This resulted in a lot of pressure on the home front too. And to work with all these great challenges, both at work and in my private life was very difficult. I was in mourning. Those I cared about most were in mourning. And at the same time, I had two children to look after.

The trigger thoughts are now just hot air

During metacognitive therapy I became aware that if
your work intrudes upon your personal life then you are
constantly analysing things. Now it became clear to me that
I had a choice. That regardless of whatever we have on our
plates, we have the right to decide how full to fill it.

This was a groundbreaking experience. I had a choice,
which was not something I had ever thought about. I agreed
with the psychologist to set a rumination time between
4.30 and 5pm every day. I was not to log thoughts which
occurred to me at other times, as the act of writing them
down would feed them. This too was groundbreaking for
me.

And the thoughts did not return. All these trigger
thoughts were just hot air!

The negative feelings I was experiencing did not
disappear. I was still insecure about the future and nervous
about not being good enough. But I was able to minimise
the processing of these thoughts.

This meant that I learned to regulate myself. I now
know that it doesn't matter a jot what experiences or
challenges I face. The point is rather how I relate to my
thoughts. Do I ruminate all day, or can I just accept and
be happy about the fact that I have chosen to leave the
rumination alone? This realisation saved me. I have no
doubt about that.

I use the strategies gained from six sessions of
metacognitive therapy on a daily basis. I know that myriad

thoughts are more likely to crop up on days when I am under a lot of pressure. Previously I would worry in advance about what these thoughts might be. I would ruminate and speculate about impressions and feelings. I don't do that anymore. I still have negative thoughts but am capable of choosing to leave them be. I know that I can avoid boarding the thought train. I have also learned that all the depressing things, all the worries and thoughts, are something that I can see through, looking beyond them to everything that really matters. The psychologist showed me this clearly by getting me to write my depressive thoughts on a windowpane and then asking me whether I could see anything behind the text on the pane. Obviously, I could do this easily. I could see shopfronts and people on the streets. This was what it was like with all my many thoughts. They are just air. I can see through them and focus on something else.

Obviously, there are still some problems or challenges which have to be solved: normal things like finances which everyone has to deal with. But once again I can just let them lie until it is the right time to think about them. I think: 'Does this have to be solved now? No, it doesn't. Okay, we'll do it at the weekend.' And so, I can just let the thought be.

On hectic days when I feel challenged, I revert to some of the exercises I was taught in the metacognitive therapy sessions. I really like the attention training with sounds (see page 83). I focus on the sounds from outside for a minute and let the trigger thoughts be. Previously it would have stressed me out if the noise from a car disturbed me while I was working or concentrating on something else. But now I know that I can also choose whether I listen to it or not.

That has to be a good thing. I think that metacognitive therapy is the reason I can still work. I'm working reduced hours, which is what I wanted. And it's going well.

BERIT'S PATH FROM TRIGGER THOUGHTS TO DEPRESSION

Berit often let herself get carried away with trigger thoughts centring on her self-esteem. She demanded of herself that everything should be perfect and that nothing should be a disappointment. Berit's trigger thoughts came most often when she thought about her work or about problems that she did not feel she had solved satisfactorily. She ruminated typically for eight hours a day, which made her depressed, tired and discouraged.

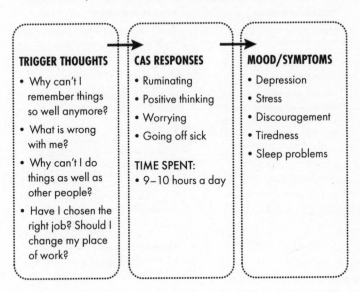

TRIGGER THOUGHTS
- Why can't I remember things so well anymore?
- What is wrong with me?
- Why can't I do things as well as other people?
- Have I chosen the right job? Should I change my place of work?

CAS RESPONSES
- Ruminating
- Positive thinking
- Worrying
- Going off sick

TIME SPENT:
- 9–10 hours a day

MOOD/SYMPTOMS
- Depression
- Stress
- Discouragement
- Tiredness
- Sleep problems

BERIT'S OLD STRATEGIES WHICH CONTRIBUTED TO HER SYMPTOMS	BERIT'S NEW STRATEGIES WHICH OVERCAME HER SYMPTOMS
Thinking style:	**Thinking style:**
When I got a trigger thought I grabbed onto it straightaway and kept on going back to the thought over and over again.	When I get a trigger thought I am aware that it can take over, and that I should let it be.
The thoughts were negative, and rumination grew to such proportions that I wasn't able to deal with it.	I bring other thoughts into play now. I look through the negative thoughts and confirm to myself that it is only a thought and that I myself can choose to what extent I want to busy myself with it or not.
Rumination could extend over a whole day or longer, and I didn't put a lid on it until I had shared my thoughts with someone else or I was completely exhausted.	I consciously postpone processing thoughts until my set rumination time.
When I shared my thoughts with others this triggered even more rumination.	I often deal with thoughts quickly instead of ruminating about them for days.
Focus for attention:	**Focus for attention:**
I focussed on my negative thoughts most of the time.	Now I stay rooted in the wider world when ruminations come knocking.
Behaviour:	**Behaviour:**
My rumination was so significant that I found it hard to spend time with other people. I became withdrawn and inward-looking.	I move around physically so as to reinforce my conscious effort to stop ruminating.
	I put music on and concentrate on the song or what is being talked about on the radio.
	I have given myself a period of time every day when I analyse my thoughts. This period of time is limited and not up for negotiation. Very often it turns out that the trigger thoughts have gone away or they are of no significance by the time I reach rumination time.

What I have learned about my thoughts:

That it is the ruminations which cause the stress or the depressive symptoms, and not the other way around.

CHAPTER 6

DOES YOUR BRAIN REALLY NEED MEDICINE?

Antidepressants can be found in many medicine cabinets all over the world. For some people, they can be the solution and a way out of sadness at a time when life feels completely unbearable. However, for many people, medication is a less satisfactory solution: only slightly effective at limiting symptoms, with negative side-effects and, often, an increased risk of relapse.

There is no shame in either seeking help for depression or in taking tablets for it. But we should, for many reasons, resist the use of antidepressants as a first course of treatment of slight or moderate depression.

New studies show that the numerous side effects of these drugs (including nausea, lack of appetite, increase in weight, dizziness and a lack of interest in sex) are seldom outweighed by their effectiveness. In cases of severe depression, medication has only shown a noticeable reduction in depressive symptoms in 50 per cent of patients. These patients also feature a high risk of relapse once they stop treatment with medication (compared to stopping treatment with therapy) because although medication treats the symptoms, it doesn't eliminate the causes of depression.

Some research has also indicated that antidepressants can increase the risk of suicidal thoughts once people stop taking the medication. The reasons for this are still not known, but one possibility is that the medication blocks the natural regulation of our feelings at the lowest level in our minds (see the S-REF model on page 11). If our negative thoughts and feelings are alleviated, suppressed or blocked by medication, this might partially explain the increased risk of relapse after stopping taking the medication.

For some people, antidepressants can seem to worsen depressive symptoms; for example, when they first start on it, some people experience strong feelings of futility and suicidal thoughts. Others say they experience new negative ruminations about their self-worth, and at the same time they are plagued with side effects such as weight gain and diminished libido. Another possible reason why medication is ineffectual for some people is that they can still ruminate and keep the depression alive, no matter how much medication they take.

If antidepressants are working for you, you are happy to take them, and you don't experience negative side effects, of course carry on taking them. I would, however, recommend that anyone consider a metacognitive therapy process either as a first step, or if you are taking medication and feel as though it isn't helping, or you're worried about its side effects.

IT'S NOT AS EASY AS SNAPPING YOUR FINGERS

Some people will say that you shouldn't ask a question like 'Does your brain really need medicine?' because medication is a great help to many people. I do not mean to say that, at the snap of your fingers, anyone could – or should – throw their pills out the window. When you stop taking medication suddenly, you risk dangerous physical side effects as well as the immediate return of depressive symptoms. If you want to stop taking antidepressants, it must always be done under the guidance of a medical professional so that you have access to help and support if the depressive symptoms return.

My mission is not to lure anyone away from medication that helps them feel better but to introduce the idea that it is possible to live without medication if they receive effective psychotherapy such as metacognitive therapy. People can learn strategies which make medication less necessary or which will eventually allow them to go without it completely.

DO YOU TAKE MEDICATION?

It is very important to emphasise that you must not suddenly stop taking medication prescribed to you. This can cause serious side effects and a relapse. If you do want to stop taking medication, I would encourage you to talk to your doctor or psychiatrist about the best way to come off it.

IS YOUR DEPRESSION CAUSED BY A LACK OF SEROTONIN?

Over time there has been an increased understanding of depression as a chemical imbalance in the brain, one which is caused by a lack of serotonin – and a corresponding increase in the belief that this deficiency should be treated with medication to increase the brain's serotonin levels. I think this is hugely problematic. It is precisely this conviction – that depression is an uncontrollable brain disorder – that keeps us in the iron grip of depression and prevents us from discovering how we can control the situation when we adopt the right mental strategies. It is true that people with depression tend to have a lower level of serotonin. But this doesn't mean we can conclude that depression is caused by this deficiency, just that the two symptoms tend to co-exist.

Depression is, as research by Wells and colleagues has shown, associated with inappropriate metacognitions and thinking strategies. We suppress, ruminate, process, monitor our mood, comfort ourselves and try to avoid uncomfortable situations. This is why, for the majority of people, the most effective treatment is less thought processing.

I often hear people with depression say that their brains have changed measurably as a result of depression – or that they believe it to have been damaged by depression. In some cases, they point to MRI scans of their brain revealing, for example, a smaller hippocampus. This is not entirely wrong. Our brains do change when we are depressed and ruminate a lot. But depression isn't the only thing to cause changes to the brain – nor are the changes necessarily permanent. The chemicals in our brain change constantly according to what we are doing; for instance, if we drink a cup of coffee or soda or eat a piece of chocolate, we can see a measurable difference in the chemical balance. This is completely normal. But even if the brain does change when we eat chocolate, we don't or can't conclude that it will cause brain damage or a permanent change. If we ruminate a lot over a long period, it will have consequences for the hormones and neurotransmitters in our brain; we might experience symptoms such as sadness and hopelessness. We might also expect our memory and concentration levels to suffer when our brains are working overtime with ruminations and worries. But our brains are plastic, and the cognitive functions will return when we stop ruminating so much.

To date, no research has shown a direct causal relationship between depression and a lack of serotonin in people's brains, whereas this connection has been shown with rumination. Several experiments have shown that when people were asked to ruminate or worry about negative thoughts, whether over a shorter or longer period, they developed symptoms of depression. In the book *Depressive Rumination* (2004), Papageorgiou and Wells describe a study which demonstrated that when you ask subjects to engage in self-focussed ruminations, such as thinking about defeat or their low mood, their depressive symptoms increase significantly. The experiment was carried out with both depressed and non-depressed people.

All in all, there is much more proof that depression is caused by inappropriate strategies such as rumination than by a chemical deficiency in the brain.

DIFFERING DEGREES OF DEPRESSION

It is paradoxical to think that many doctors and psychiatrists continue to prefer anti-depression medication as the first step in fighting depression when we now know that effective psychotherapy is vital to achieve lasting effects. I am convinced that doctors prescribe medication in good faith and that they only want to help their patients. The fact that so many prescriptions are written every single day is down to, and reinforces, the widespread notion that depression is an illness and that medication is a faster and therefore less expensive treatment than psychotherapy. In some countries and regions where referring patients for therapy can involve long waiting times, prescribing antidepressants may also be the only option for doctors to provide immediate treatment.

There is, however, nothing to indicate that medication is less costly than metacognitive therapy – and certainly not in the longer term. The effective long-term way out of depression is to learn better strategies for dealing with internal and external challenges in life. Metacognitive therapy may be the most sustainable solution to depression.

My studies with Professor Wells and other studies show that people typically recover from depression after six to twelve sessions of metacognitive therapy – this also applies to more severe cases. In contrast to medication, it has no side effects, and it does not take months or years like other treatment options.

Once in a while, I encounter clients who continue with their medication even after going through a metacognitive treatment process and overcoming their depression because they wonder: 'What if it is helping me? What happens if I find I can't manage without it?'

I understand this concern and reiterate that people should only stop their medication when they feel they have sufficient control over their ruminations and day to day life, and then only after they have made a gradual reduction plan with their doctor.

But if people continue too long on medication without being depressed, and after they have learned the metacognitive strategies, they will undermine that feeling of self-control. It is a bit like continuing to ride a bike with stabilisers on, long after you have learned to ride.

TAKE OFF THE STABILISERS

Depression typically also leads to a worsening of cognitive functions, particularly the ability to concentrate and remember. Many people find that they forget appointments, birthdays and everyday tasks. Concentration and memory problems are a very common consequence of CAS and can be very frustrating. Suddenly we can no longer concentrate on our favourite series or the novel we were reading.

It can be tempting to introduce stabiliser-type strategies, such as lots of daily notes to ourselves about all the things we need to remember. This would be doing us a disservice because these notes can increase stress and affirm the idea that there is something wrong with our memory. Cognitive problems are typically a consequence of too much thinking. If we are using our heads all the time, then they will not function optimally. It's the equivalent of a professional football player playing football day and night and never taking time to recover. Taking a break from thinking in the form of detached mindfulness is important for our heads to function optimally.

My experience shows that when we begin to ruminate less, mental performance, concentration and memory will gradually return. The memory – like the body and the mind – can heal itself.

TAKING TIME OFF SICK CAN EXTEND DEPRESSION

In our society we often advise people with depression to take time off sick from work, to recharge their batteries, so as to overcome the depression. I often have clients who, at the start of their sick leave, have been told by health professionals that they should get some peace and quiet and do as little as possible. When I ask clients if this helped their depressive symptoms, the answer most often is no. For some people, a period of sick leave brings some peace and therefore relief. This applies, for example, for deeply depressed people who may need a break from external triggers. It is sometimes easier to think less at home on the sofa than in a busy workplace. Taking time off sick can therefore be a useful short-term aid, but it is not a solution in itself as it doesn't alter the mechanisms that are the driving forces behind our symptoms. When you take sick leave, you are put into a temporarily protected situation which does not contribute to you learning how to manage at work, and it may decrease your sense of control over your life. Moreover, people who have taken time off sick with depression risk relapsing as soon as they are back in the environment where the trigger thoughts occur, for example the workplace, if they have not learned to observe trigger thoughts passively and avoid ruminating.

Another reason why some of my clients experience a worsening of their depression when they take time off sick is that they have extra time in which to ruminate. If you have nothing else to do but sit on the sofa and stare into space, then you risk ruminating yourself further into depression.

When the same people begin to do something and steer their thoughts away from their problems, they report that their mood improves. Depression eases when you stop ruminating. You cannot, therefore, relax yourself out of depression. You cannot sleep your way out of it. You will just end up becoming more lethargic.

A man started therapy with me recently. After a long period during which he experienced low mood, loss of appetite and a lack of energy, he was given sick leave from his job as an auditor. The sick leave did not improve his mood. He began to speculate about whether he would ever be well again, and what other people thought about him and his situation. In addition to ruminating, he began to avoid social occasions since he dreaded questions about his work situation. Slowly, his ruminations and his attempts to avoid people and get-togethers led to a worsening of his symptoms. He did not get better. When he started metacognitive therapy, he discovered that he could reduce his CAS responses at home, in social situations and in the workplace, and his positivity and good mood returned. He knew now that he had full control over the old strategies which were causing his symptoms.

CHAPTER 7

END DEPRESSION
FOR GOOD

I would like this book to inspire people to free themselves from sadness and depression. By discovering trigger thoughts and choosing to get off the rumination train, no matter which station we have reached, we can overcome depression. To do this we need to change the metacognitive beliefs which govern our thought processes, and we need to practise limiting ruminations, regardless of whether they are about minor everyday triggers, such as small family conflicts, or more intense matters, such as illness, death or divorce.

Remember, our thoughts do not themselves know if they are worth two minutes or five hours of rumination. It is *we* who undertake this evaluation. It is only us. When we practise engaging with our thoughts and feelings less and instead choose to focus on other things – such as a book, a bike ride or the people around us – we will find that we move out of our heads and into our lives. This does not just lessen depressive symptoms but also increases quality of life. We do well when we can become engrossed in time with our children, read a good book or watch a TV show, regardless of whether we have negative or positive thoughts and feelings.

Life is lived in the wider world, outside of ourselves. It is not a matter of distracting ourselves in order to avoid negative thoughts and feelings. It is about letting our minds engage with life.

Sadness, anger and sorrow are all a part of life that none of us can escape. But, with the right awareness and more detached mindfulness, we can learn how to avoid deepening and nurturing negative feelings, and they will begin to regulate themselves. The mind heals itself under the right conditions.

Our brain functions best with measured doses of thinking. Breaks and recovery time allow us to function optimally and also to think creatively. If we are to come up with our best ideas, our brain needs daily rest. I'm not talking about sleep here, just off-periods –a sort of mental screen break where we let thoughts come and go without interacting with them.

Detached mindfulness is our brain's breathing space. Here we go into 'pause mode' and let the lowest level in our mind regulate itself (see the S-REF model, page 11). We can see that the brain doesn't stop producing thoughts just because we refrain from processing them. But we will notice that fewer or different thoughts come. This is because our metacognitive assistant works best if we are not continually pressing it to find answers. We gain more positivity and energy and become more creative when we ruminate less. Therefore, it is a good idea to take a break with detached mindfulness during the day. We can sit on the sofa and look out of the window. We can watch a good film. Or we can just enjoy being with family or friends.

I am aware that the messages in this book are controversial since they require a complete change in our understanding of the causes of and treatment for depression. The majority of psychiatric treatments for depression involve you seeing yourself as particularly vulnerable, and so taking medication or protecting yourself from situations which can trigger stress and lead to depression. Our society is wedded to the idea of processing: talking through or analysing negative thoughts and feelings caused by life crises. So, I understand if you feel provoked by the fact that I am advocating the opposite.

The World Health Organisation (WHO) anticipates that depression will become one of the greatest challenges facing humankind by 2025. This would be a terrible state of affairs for the individuals suffering, as well as for society as a whole. But depression is not a chronic, incurable condition, and with metacognitive therapy we can alter this course. Of people using metacognitive techniques, 70–80 per cent can overcome depression completely, without using antidepressants or traditional cognitive and analytical therapies; this is a markedly better success rate than for other tested treatments for depression.

REGRETS ABOUT LOST YEARS

When we ruminate less and are more present in the outside world, we will find we have more time and more positivity.

I often meet people who have spent huge amounts of time speculating, which has led to wasted chances, diminished quality of life and depression. It can cause these individuals great sorrow to recognise that they have missed out on many opportunities and good times.

It is also natural for this sense of loss to inspire new trigger thoughts: 'Why have I wasted so many years of my life? If only I had known this before – I could have saved myself from depression, years of therapy, pills and admissions.'

Not much can be done about the wasted years. The past cannot be relived, and the years will not come back by ruminating about them. We should not beat ourselves up about it. We deal with everything using the knowledge that we have at a given time. We could, therefore, conclude that we had good reason to act as we did. But it's best not to go into the past too deeply. Instead, now is the time to look forward and to reach out for the hope of a future without depression, which metacognitive therapy can provide.

My hope is that this book inspires you to seek out metacognitive therapy, so that you can learn to deal with your negative thoughts and feelings. The method requires practice and support from a qualified treatment provider to be most successful. While the method is new, it is becoming more accessible around the world as the number of trained therapists increases. You can find a list of registered therapists and their contact details at the MCT Institute's website:

https://mct-institute.co.uk/mct-registered-therapists.

You can gain positive experiences and successes with this method that will change your self-image. You can see yourself as a strong and robust person who has full control over how you deal with thoughts and feelings. You can learn to rely on your skills to get through emotional experiences without always being sad, down or depressed.

Regardless of which or how many trigger thoughts we are affected by, and regardless of how unhappy, frustrated or sorrowful we become as a result of life's difficulties, we can deal with them all with detached mindfulness.

Adrian Wells said to me once: 'Trigger thoughts are like fishhooks, and you are the fish who comes swimming along. You cannot decide how many fish hooks you encounter, but you can decide whether you swim past them or take the bait.' It is impossible to avoid trigger thoughts as you go through life. And sometimes we cannot avoid biting. But with metacognitive therapy we can learn to keep swimming and appreciate the world around us, even if the stream is full of trigger thoughts. We can learn to pass the hooks by and even to get ourselves back off the hook, without using up our strength in suppressing thoughts or forcing them to go away. We can learn to continue with our lives.

I usually give my clients an extra challenge if they are impatient and want to control their ruminations quickly. I challenge them to jump into life: to go on new adventures and dare to look for experiences which they know might give rise to trigger thoughts. I say to them that now might be the time to have that difficult conversation with the boss. To find a new job. To move out of the area they have had enough of. The more experiences we busy ourselves with and the more we jump straight to action, the more we will chase away the ruminations and feel in control. This creates a positive spiral which makes us more resilient and better able to fend off long-term sadness and depression.

▶ This is what I do in my clinic:

HOW TO BECOME A METAMASTER

The belief that we can control our ruminations comes with experience. You cannot learn to ride a bike simply by reading a book. You also need to practise. It is not until you believe that you can ride on two wheels without falling off that you will be able to do so.

I often use this metaphor when I speak to clients about how to play the part of a 'metamaster': a person who has mastered the ability to discover their trigger thoughts, control their ruminations and practise detached mindfulness.

I ask my clients to practise – again and again. I suggest that that they take a few minutes every day to practise discovering their trigger thoughts and to control their ruminations with the help of detached mindfulness. Life continually presents us with experiences that cause trigger thoughts. When the client feels confident using detached mindfulness, they can challenge themselves to face situations that cause trigger thoughts, such as:

- Striking up a debate with a family member, who tends to get into heated discussions.

- Asking the boss for a salary increase.

- Asking someone out on a date.

- Doing something out of the ordinary and
  spontaneous.

The more experience we have of controlling our responses to trig-ger thoughts, the more we will believe we are in control. And the more we believe we are in control, the more able we will be to control our responses. We should not avoid life but practise deal-ing with it, every single day.

'Thoughts don't matter but your response to them does.'

ADRIAN WELLS

GET TO KNOW THE CONCEPTS

Attention training technique (ATT) is an awareness exercise that shows that we can shift our attention, independent of inner events (thoughts and feelings) and outer events (the world around us).

CAS (cognitive attentional syndrome) is a collection of strategies which, when used frequently, will backfire and keep depression alive. These include ruminations, worries, mood monitoring and other inappropriate coping strategies.

Detached mindfulness is a passive awareness of your thought stream. It is the opposite of ruminating.

Metacognitive beliefs are your conceptions of your own thoughts and thought processes, in other words, the thoughts you have about your thoughts. Our metacognitive knowledge and beliefs control, for example, how long we choose to ruminate over trigger thoughts. If we do not believe that we have control over this, it is difficult to limit rumination times.

Rumination is our thought processing. It is a strategy that aims to create order and to find solutions to our problems by mulling over thoughts and ideas at length. The issue is that excessive rumination can have the opposite effect. If we allow ourselves to be tempted to jump on our trigger-thought trains, then we will ruminate constantly, our mood will deteriorate, and we will most probably develop depressive symptoms, which we can foster for years.

The **Self-Regulatory Executive Function Model (S-REF)** is Wells and Matthews' (1994) metacognitive model of the structure and self-regulation of the mind. It includes three levels, from the lower level, which is constantly hit by impulses, thoughts and feelings, to the middle level, where we strategize how to deal with our thoughts, to the upper, metacognitive level, which is our knowledge of possible strategies.

Trigger thoughts are thoughts which have the potential to turn into ruminations. They are typically intensely emotional thoughts. Whether they develop into ruminations depends on whether or not we process them.

WOULD YOU LIKE TO TRY METACOGNITIVE THERAPY?

Metacognitive therapy is an effective short-term treatment for poor mental health. The method has been shown to have very good results. Over six to twelve sessions with a metacognitive therapist, you will learn the principles of the therapy and go through each stage of the method. Around 70–80 per cent will recover from depressive symptoms.

I am concerned with maintaining professionalism within metacognitive therapy and therefore recommend that anyone who would like to take part in a group programme or 1:1 session chooses a qualified therapist to get the best result.

In recent years, Professor Hans Nordahl and the method's creator Professor Adrian Wells have been training and certifying new therapists at the MCT Institute in Denmark. Only about 60 per cent of trainees pass this course, become certified and thus can use the designation 'MCT Institute registered therapist'. You will get the best metacognitive treatment from a psychologist who is MCT-I registered.

You can see a list of MCT-I registered practitioners near you here:

https://mct-institute.co.uk/
mct-registered-therapists

If you are unable to find a therapist near to you, bear in mind that some clinics are able to provide online therapy in English, so it's worth exploring those options.

If you are a mental health care professional and are interested in training in MCT, you may find the treatment manual useful (Wells, 2009). You can find more information about training here:

https://mct-institute.co.uk/mct-master-class

REFERENCES

Callesen, P., Jensen, A.B. & Wells, A. (2014). 'Metacognitive
Therapy in Recurrent Depression: A Case Replication Series
in Denmark'. *Scandinavian Journal of Psychology* 55(1): 60–64.

Cuijpers P., Hollon S.D., van Straten A., Bockting, C., Berking,
M. & Andersson, G. (2013). 'Does cognitive behaviour therapy
have an enduring effect that is superior to keeping patients
on continuation pharmacotherapy? A meta-analysis'. *BMJ*
Open 3: e002542.

Dammen, T., Papageorgiou, C. & Wells, A. (2015). 'An Open
Trial of Group Metacognitive Therapy for Depression in
Norway'. *Nordic Journal of Psychiatry* 69(2): 126–31.

Diagnostic and Statistical Manual of Mental Disorders: DSM-5 (2013).
Washington, D.C.: American Psychiatric Association.

Hagen, R., Hjemdal, O., Solem, S., Kennair, L.E.O., Nordahl,
H.M., Fisher, P. & Wells, A. (2017). 'Metacognitive Therapy for
Depression in Adults: A Waiting List Randomized Controlled
Trial with Six Months Follow-Up'. *Frontiers in Psychology* 8:31.

Hollon, S.D., DeRubeis, J., Shelton, C., Amsterdam, D.,
Salomon, R., O'Reardon, J., Lovett, M., Young, P., Haman,
K., Freeman, B. & Gallop, R. (2005). 'Prevention of Relapse
Following Cognitive Therapy vs Medications in Moderate to
Severe Depression'. *Arch Gen Psychiatry* 62(4): 417–22.

Jordan, J., Carter, J.D., McIntosh, V.V., Fernando, K., Frampton,
C.M., Porter, R.J., Mulder, R.T., Lacey, C. & Joyce, P.R.
(2014). 'Metacognitive Therapy Versus Cognitive Behavioural
Therapy for Depression: A Randomized Pilot Study'. *Australian
and New Zealand Journal of Psychiatry* 48 (10): 932–43.

Kirsch, I. (2009). 'Antidepressants and the Placebo Response'.
Epidemiology and Psychiatric Sciences 18(4): 318–22.

Normann, N., Emmerik, A.A. & Morina, N. (2014). 'The Efficacy of Metacognitive Therapy for Anxiety and Depression: A Meta-Analytic Review'. *Depression and Anxiety*, 31(5): 402–11.

Papageorgiou, C. & Wells, A. (2014). 'Group Metacognitive Therapy for Severe Antidepressant and CBT Resistant Depression: A Baseline-Controlled Trial'. *Cognitive Therapy and Research* 39(1): 14–22.

Papageorgiou, C. & Wells, A. (2004). *Depressive Rumination: Nature, Theory and Treatment*: John Wiley & Sons.

Papageorgiou, C. & Wells, A. (2003). 'An Empirical Test of a Clinical Metacognitive Model of Rumination and Depression'. *Cognitive Therapy and Research* 27(3): 261–73.

Papageorgiou, C. & Wells, A. (2000). 'Treatment of Recurrent Major Depression with Attention Training'. *Cognitive and Behavioral Practice* 7(4): 407–13.

Turner, E.H., Matthews, A.M., Linardatos, E., Tell, R.A. & Rosenthal, R. (2008). 'Selective Publication of Antidepressant Trials and its Influence on Apparent Efficacy'. *New England Journal of Medicine* 358(3): 252–60.

Wells, A. (2009). *Metacognitive Therapy for Anxiety and Depression*. New York: Guilford Press.

Wells, A. (2007). 'The Attention Training Technique: Theory, Effects and a Metacognitive Hypothesis on Auditory Hallucinations'. *Cognitive and Behavioural Practice* 14: 134–8.

Wells, A. (2005). 'Detached Mindfulness in Cognitive Therapy: A Metacognitive Analysis and Ten Techniques'. *Journal of Rational-Emotive and Cognitive-Behavior Therapy* 23(4): 337–55.

Wells, A. (2000). *Emotional Disorders and Metacognition: Innovative Cognitive Therapy*. Chichester, UK: Wiley.

Wells, A. & Fisher, P. (2016). *Treating Depression: MCT, CBT and Third Wave Therapies*. Chichester, UK: Wiley-Blackwell.

Wells, A., Fisher, P., Myers, S., Wheatley, J., Patel, T. & Brewin, C.R. (2012). 'Metacognitive Therapy in Treatment-Resistant

Depression: A Platform Trial'. *Behaviour Research and Therapy* 50(6): 367–73.

Wells, A., Fisher, P., Myers, S., Wheatley, J., Patel, T. & Brewin, C.R. (2009). 'Metacognitive Therapy in Recurrent and Persistent Depression: A Multiple-Baseline Study of a New Treatment'. *Cognitive Therapy and Research* 33(3): 291–300.

Wells, A. & Matthews, G. (1996). 'Modelling Cognition in Emotional Disorder: The S-REF Model'. *Behaviour Research and Therapy* 34(11): 881–8.

Wells, A. & Matthews, G. (1994). *Attention and Emotion: A Clinical Perspective*. Hove, UK: Erlbaum.